Unlock the Path on Online Income Without Fees:

Your Ultimate Guide to Financial Freedom

Sam Fried

Author's Note:

Dear Reader,

Welcome to "**Unlock the Path to Online Income Without Fees: Your Ultimate Guide to Financial Freedom**." This book is the culmination of a deep exploration into the world of online income and aims to serve as your compass in navigating the realm of financial opportunities without the hindrance of initial fees.

In a world increasingly shaped by digital landscapes, the potential for earning money online is vast, diverse, and often clouded by misconceptions. The inspiration behind this book stems from the desire to demystify the notion that making money online demands significant upfront investments. I firmly believe that with the right guidance and strategies, financial success in the online sphere can be achieved without the barrier of initial costs.

Throughout these pages, my goal is to provide you with a comprehensive roadmap, a blueprint that not only introduces you to various online income streams but also offers actionable insights and practical advice. Each chapter is meticulously crafted to shed light on a specific avenue for generating income, guiding you through the process, and equipping you with the tools needed to succeed.

The book covers a wide spectrum of opportunities, from freelancing and e-commerce to affiliate marketing, content creation, and various other lucrative fields. It explores lesser-known yet promising areas such as remote work, cryptocurrency trading, and print-on-demand services, all with an emphasis on how you can initiate these endeavors without any initial financial burden.

Moreover, I've endeavored to encompass a variety of skills and interests, ensuring that there's something for everyone within these pages. Whether you're an aspiring entrepreneur, a creative mind, a tech enthusiast, or someone seeking a side income, the goal is to empower you with the knowledge to take that crucial first step towards financial freedom.

I understand that beginning a journey into online income can be both exciting and daunting. That's why this book not only provides insights but also encourages reflection. The closing chapters are designed to prompt you to contemplate what you've learned and to chart your course forward. I believe that your success is not just about the information in these pages but also about the action you take based on this knowledge.

In closing, I want to express my sincerest wish that this book becomes a beacon of inspiration and guidance as you navigate the path to financial freedom. I hope it emboldens you to explore, innovate, and seize the myriad opportunities awaiting you in the online sphere.

Best wishes on your journey,

[Sam Fried]

Copyright

Table of Content

About the Book

In today's digital age, the potential for generating income online is vast and diverse. "Unlock the Path to Online Income Without Fees" offers a comprehensive and detailed roadmap to tapping into these opportunities without any initial investment.

Spanning 30 chapters, this guide navigates the intricacies of various online income streams, debunking the myth that making money online necessitates significant upfront costs. Each chapter provides a deep dive into different avenues for generating income, offering practical insights and strategies for success.

The journey begins with an exploration of freelancing fundamentals, shedding light on how to kickstart a freelance career in different fields without incurring any fees. It then moves on to the world of e-commerce, guiding readers through setting up online stores, dropshipping, and selling products without any initial investment.

Affiliate marketing, blogging, content creation, and monetization strategies are thoroughly explored, offering valuable insights into leveraging platforms like YouTube, podcasts, and more to generate revenue without upfront expenses.

From online surveys and market research to online tutoring, the book illuminates various opportunities for earning money without the need for an initial investment. It covers virtual assistance, remote work, cryptocurrency and online trading, and even delves into the possibilities of building a social media presence for income without any upfront costs.

Readers are introduced to the world of creating and selling digital products, print-on-demand services, gaming and eSports earnings, and even avenues like stock photography and art sales – all without initial expenses.

The guide further explores opportunities in web development, mobile apps, podcasting, SEO, and digital marketing, elucidating how individuals can tap into these fields for financial gain without incurring fees.

Remote data entry, writing and publishing, language teaching, and online real estate opportunities are all detailed within these pages, offering a wide array of options for generating income online without any upfront costs.

Moreover, the book covers areas such as virtual assistant development, building and monetizing online communities, fundraising, and crowdfunding initiatives, catering to a diverse range of interests and skill sets.

Lastly, it explores the future landscape of AI, virtual assistant development, remote health and wellness services, and how individuals can leverage these emerging opportunities for financial gain without the need for initial expenses.

"Unlock the Path to Online Income Without Fees" is not just a mere guide but a comprehensive manual designed to equip readers with the necessary tools and insights to embark on their journey toward financial independence. It provides reflection points and guidance for the next steps, ensuring that individuals, regardless of their expertise or familiarity with the online sphere, can step into the world of online income generation without any financial barriers.

For anyone seeking to explore the potential of online income without the burden of initial fees, this book serves as a valuable companion, offering knowledge, strategies, and inspiration to unlock the doors to financial abundance in the digital realm.

Chapter 1: Introduction to Online Earning

In the age of digital innovation and connectivity, the concept of earning money online has become an increasingly popular and viable option for many individuals seeking financial independence, flexibility, and new opportunities. The internet has transformed the way we work, creating a vast landscape of possibilities that extend far beyond the confines of traditional employment. This shift has empowered people to explore alternative avenues of income, allowing them to leverage their skills, creativity, and entrepreneurship in the virtual sphere.

The allure of online earning is multifaceted. It offers a diverse range of options that cater to various interests, expertise, and preferences. Whether one is looking to supplement their existing income, transition to remote work, or even establish a full-fledged online career, the digital realm provides a platform for achieving these aspirations.

The landscape of online earning is expansive and constantly evolving. It encompasses numerous strategies, business models, and platforms. From freelancing and content creation to e-commerce, affiliate marketing, online courses, and more, the opportunities are as diverse as the people who pursue them.

One of the fundamental advantages of online earning is its flexibility. Traditional nine-to-five jobs often come with rigid schedules, fixed locations, and limited autonomy. However, the online sphere breaks these barriers, allowing individuals to work from anywhere, at any time, and on projects they find meaningful and enjoyable. This flexibility not only offers a better work-life balance but also empowers individuals to tailor their schedules according to their personal preferences.

The internet has democratized earning potential, providing access to a global audience. With a laptop and internet connection, individuals can reach customers, clients, or audiences worldwide, transcending geographical boundaries. This connectivity not only widens the market but also fosters cultural exchange and collaboration on an unprecedented scale.

Moreover, the low barriers to entry in the online space make it accessible to nearly anyone willing to learn, adapt, and put in the effort. Many online earning avenues do not require substantial upfront investments or specialized degrees. Instead, they rely on skills, dedication, and a willingness to learn and adapt to the rapidly changing digital landscape.

However, while the realm of online earning offers incredible potential, it is not without its challenges. The digital space is highly competitive, demanding continuous innovation, adaptability, and a deep understanding of the evolving trends. Navigating the complexities of online algorithms, understanding audience behavior, and staying updated with technology advancements are crucial for success.

The abundance of options in online earning can also be overwhelming. Choosing the right path requires a deep understanding of one's skills, interests, and market demand. It demands careful research, strategic planning, and sometimes trial and error to find the most suitable avenue.

Furthermore, the lack of guaranteed stability and the presence of scams or unreliable sources pose risks that individuals must navigate. Building a reliable income stream online often takes time, effort, and persistence. It requires a combination of skill development, networking, consistent effort, and sometimes a bit of luck.

In this journey of exploring the vast landscape of online earning, this guide aims to provide insights, tips, and strategies that can serve as a compass, guiding individuals through the intricacies of the digital realm. Whether one is a freelancer, an aspiring entrepreneur, an artist, or someone simply curious about the potentials of online earning, the chapters that follow will delve deeper into specific avenues, strategies, and best practices to empower and equip individuals on their online earning journey.

Chapter by chapter, we'll explore various online earning avenues, diving into the intricacies of each method, understanding the prerequisites, and uncovering the strategies that can help individuals succeed. From mastering the art of freelancing and navigating the world of content creation to establishing an e-commerce empire or creating and marketing online courses, this guide will serve as a comprehensive resource to equip and inspire individuals in their pursuit of online financial independence.

So, let us embark on this journey through the digital landscape, where innovation, creativity, and determination intersect, paving the way for new opportunities and the realization of individual aspirations in the realm of online earning.

Chapter 2: Freelancing Fundamentals

Freelancing, in its essence, embodies the freedom and flexibility that many seek in their professional lives. It's a way of working that transcends traditional office structures, enabling individuals to ply their trade or offer their expertise without the confines of a fixed workplace. In today's dynamic work landscape, freelancing has emerged as a viable and popular means of employment for millions worldwide.

The journey of a freelancer is often an amalgamation of independence, entrepreneurial spirit, and adaptability. It's a lifestyle choice that offers an array of opportunities, yet demands a unique set of skills and mindset. While it can be incredibly rewarding, it also presents its own challenges and uncertainties.

At its core, freelancing encompasses a diverse array of professions and skills. From writers and designers to programmers, marketers, consultants, and beyond, the scope of freelance work is vast. This diversity lends itself to various platforms and marketplaces where freelancers can showcase their talents and connect with potential clients or employers.

One of the fundamental aspects of freelancing is the autonomy it offers. Freelancers have the liberty to set their schedules, choose their projects, and often work from anywhere. This flexibility is a cornerstone of the freelance lifestyle, allowing individuals to balance work with personal commitments and preferences. It's not uncommon for freelancers to work during non-traditional hours, catering to global clients across different time zones.

However, with freedom comes responsibility. Freelancers must manage their time efficiently, handle their finances, market their services, negotiate contracts, and ensure the quality of their work. Essentially, they are the CEOs of their own businesses. This demands a keen sense of self-discipline, business acumen, and the ability to adapt to ever-changing market demands.

Building a successful freelance career requires more than just skills in one's chosen field. A freelancer must possess a multifaceted skill set, often far beyond their core expertise. Communication, negotiation, marketing, project management, and self-promotion are crucial in establishing a thriving freelance business. The ability to network, build relationships, and maintain a stellar reputation is paramount in a landscape where word-of-mouth and referrals often dictate success.

Furthermore, navigating the financial aspect of freelancing is fundamental. Understanding how to price services, manage cash flow, budget, and plan for taxes are critical components of sustaining a freelancing career. Unlike traditional employment, freelancers are responsible for their own benefits, such as healthcare and retirement planning, which adds another layer of complexity to their financial considerations.

Technology has significantly influenced the landscape of freelancing. Online platforms, marketplaces, and social media have democratized the playing field, allowing freelancers to access a global pool of clients and opportunities. Digital tools and platforms have streamlined communication, project management, and financial transactions, making it easier for freelancers to operate efficiently from anywhere in the world.

The journey of a freelancer is not devoid of challenges. Inconsistent income, the need for constant self-promotion, the isolation of working alone, and the lack of traditional job security are common hurdles. Managing multiple projects, clients, and deadlines while maintaining a work-life balance can also be demanding. However, the freedom and flexibility often outweigh these challenges for many, making freelancing a highly desirable career choice.

Successful freelancers develop a niche and build a brand around their expertise. Specialization in a particular area often leads to better opportunities and higher rates. Consistent quality, meeting deadlines, and providing excellent customer service become the pillars of their reputation, leading to recurring clients and referrals.

Networking is a vital aspect of a freelancer's success. Building relationships with other freelancers, industry professionals, and potential clients can open doors to new opportunities. Attending industry events, utilizing social media, and participating in online forums or groups related to one's field can foster connections and collaborations.

Continuous learning and adaptation are essential for a freelancer to stay relevant in a rapidly evolving market. Keeping up with industry trends, updating skills, and being open to new technologies and methodologies are crucial for sustained success.

In conclusion, freelancing represents a unique and increasingly popular approach to work. It offers unparalleled freedom and flexibility, allowing individuals to craft their professional lives on their terms. However, this freedom comes with the responsibility of managing various aspects of a business, including marketing, finance, and client relations. Success in freelancing demands a combination of expertise in one's field, business acumen, adaptability, and a commitment to continuous improvement. While it presents its challenges, freelancing remains an enticing career choice for those seeking autonomy and the ability to shape their own professional destinies.

Chapter 3: E-commerce Ventures

In the modern age, where convenience and accessibility are paramount, the digital landscape has witnessed a tremendous transformation. The rise of e-commerce ventures has redefined the way we shop, connect, and do business. This phenomenon has reshaped not only our daily routines but also the very structure of the global economy. As we delve into the intricate world of e-commerce ventures, we will explore the evolution of this industry, its impact on society and business, and the various factors that contribute to its success.

1. The Dawn of E-commerce

E-commerce, short for electronic commerce, refers to the buying and selling of goods and services over the internet. It encompasses a vast array of transactions, from online retail stores and marketplaces to digital payment systems and B2B (business-to-business) commerce. The concept of e-commerce is not a recent one, but its exponential growth and technological advancement in recent decades have propelled it into the forefront of global business.

The roots of e-commerce can be traced back to the 1960s and 1970s when electronic data interchange (EDI) was introduced, allowing businesses to exchange information electronically. However, it was not until the 1990s that the world witnessed the birth of the modern e-commerce industry. The launch of Amazon in 1995, an online bookstore at its inception, marked a pivotal moment in the history of e-commerce. Amazon's success paved the way for other e-commerce ventures, and the industry has been growing ever since.

2. The E-commerce Landscape Today

Fast forward to today, and e-commerce has transformed into a massive global industry with a diverse array of players. The e-commerce ecosystem includes online marketplaces, traditional retailers with online stores, direct-to-consumer brands, e-commerce platforms, payment gateways, and logistics providers, among others. Some of the key players in the global e-commerce industry include Amazon, Alibaba, eBay, Shopify, and many others.

This ever-expanding landscape is driven by a myriad of factors, the first and foremost being the increasing internet penetration and the proliferation of mobile devices. The ease of access to the internet and the availability of smartphones have made it possible for billions of people worldwide to connect and conduct business online. This ubiquity has democratized commerce, enabling small businesses and individuals to participate in the global marketplace.

3. The Impact on Traditional Retail

The rapid growth of e-commerce ventures has had a profound impact on traditional retail. Brick-and-mortar stores are no longer the sole destination for shoppers. E-commerce has provided consumers with the convenience of browsing and purchasing products from the comfort of their homes. The traditional retail sector has had to adapt and innovate to survive in this digital era.

Many retailers have embraced an omnichannel approach, combining physical stores with e-commerce platforms to offer a seamless shopping experience. E-commerce has also forced retailers to rethink their supply chain management and logistics. The need for efficient order fulfillment and last-mile delivery has become crucial to meet customer expectations in the age of e-commerce.

4. Consumer Behavior and Expectations

E-commerce has not only transformed the way businesses operate but has also significantly influenced consumer behavior and expectations. The convenience of online shopping, with features like one-click ordering, personalized recommendations, and user-friendly interfaces, has set a new standard for customer experience.

Consumers now expect a seamless and hassle-free shopping process, from the moment they land on an e-commerce website to the post-purchase support. This has put pressure on e-commerce ventures to continually innovate and improve their services. It has also necessitated a focus on data analytics and customer insights to better understand and cater to consumer preferences.

5. Technological Advancements

One of the driving forces behind the success of e-commerce ventures is the continuous advancement of technology. Innovations in payment processing, security, data analytics, and artificial intelligence have all played a significant role in shaping the industry.

Payment gateways and digital wallets have made online transactions more secure and convenient. Machine learning algorithms have been employed for personalized product recommendations and optimizing supply chain operations. Chatbots and virtual assistants have improved customer support and engagement. Augmented reality (AR) and virtual reality (VR) technologies have enhanced the online shopping experience by allowing customers to visualize products in their real-world environments before making a purchase.

6. Challenges and Competition

The growth of e-commerce ventures has not been without its fair share of challenges and competition. While it presents numerous opportunities, it also introduces a competitive landscape where businesses must constantly adapt and innovate to stay relevant.

Competition in the e-commerce space is fierce. Large corporations like Amazon and Alibaba dominate the global market, but there is still ample room for smaller, niche e-commerce ventures to thrive. Differentiation and brand identity are key factors for success. Businesses need to find their unique value proposition and effectively communicate it to their target audience.

Cybersecurity is another pressing concern. As e-commerce transactions involve the exchange of sensitive personal and financial information, there is a constant need to protect against data breaches and fraud. Security measures and compliance with data protection regulations are non-negotiable for e-commerce ventures.

7. Regulatory and Legal Challenges

E-commerce ventures operate in a complex regulatory environment. They must comply with a variety of laws and regulations, which can vary significantly from one region to another. Taxation, data privacy, consumer protection, and intellectual property are some of the areas where e-commerce businesses must navigate complex legal frameworks.

Taxation is a particularly thorny issue. Cross-border e-commerce transactions can be subject to a web of different tax regimes. E-commerce platforms and sellers must be aware of and adhere to these regulations to avoid legal complications.

Data privacy is also a matter of concern, with the General Data Protection Regulation (GDPR) in Europe and various data protection laws in other regions imposing strict requirements on how personal data is handled. E-commerce businesses must invest in data security and transparency to maintain consumer trust.

8. The Role of Logistics

Efficient logistics and supply chain management are paramount in the success of e-commerce ventures. The promise of quick and reliable delivery is a significant driver of customer satisfaction. This has led to the rise of third-party logistics providers (3PLs) and the development of innovative fulfillment strategies.

Warehousing and fulfillment centers have become central to the e-commerce ecosystem. E-commerce businesses are increasingly outsourcing their storage and order fulfillment operations to 3PLs. These providers specialize in efficient storage and order processing, allowing e-commerce companies to focus on their core competencies.

Additionally, the concept of same-day or next-day delivery, made possible by strategically located fulfillment centers, has become a competitive advantage. Companies like Amazon have pioneered this approach, setting high standards for delivery speed and reliability.

27

9. The International Expansion of E-commerce

E-commerce has transcended borders, enabling businesses to reach a global customer base. Cross-border e-commerce, also known as international e-commerce, has become a significant driver of economic growth. It allows businesses to tap into new markets and consumers to access a wider range of products and services.

The international expansion of e-commerce, however, comes with its own set of challenges. These include understanding and complying with the regulations of different countries, dealing with currency exchange rates, navigating language and cultural differences, and addressing the complexities of international shipping and customs clearance.

10. Sustainability and E-commerce

As the world grapples with environmental challenges, the sustainability of e-commerce practices has come into focus. The rapid growth of online shopping has raised concerns about the carbon footprint of delivery logistics and the environmental impact of packaging materials.

E-commerce ventures are increasingly adopting eco-friendly practices to address these concerns. This includes exploring greener packaging solutions, optimizing delivery routes to reduce emissions, and investing in renewable energy to power their operations. Additionally, some businesses are focusing on creating a more sustainable product lifecycle, from sourcing raw materials to the end-of-life disposal.

11. The Future of E-commerce Ventures

The e-commerce industry is in a state of continuous evolution. Looking to the future, several trends are expected to shape the landscape of e-commerce ventures. The integration of artificial intelligence and machine learning is anticipated to further personalize the shopping experience and streamline operations. Voice commerce, facilitated by virtual assistants and smart speakers, is also expected to gain traction.

Furthermore, the metaverse, a collective virtual shared space, is increasingly becoming a topic of interest for e-commerce. As virtual reality and augmented reality technologies advance, the metaverse could provide new avenues for immersive shopping experiences and social interactions, blurring the lines between physical and digital retail.

Additionally, sustainability and ethical practices are likely to become more embedded in the e-commerce industry. Consumers are becoming more conscious of the environmental and social impact of their purchases. Businesses that prioritize sustainability and social responsibility are poised to gain a competitive edge.

In conclusion, e-commerce ventures have revolutionized the way we shop, conduct business, and interact with the global marketplace. The industry's growth and success are driven by technological innovation, changing consumer behavior, and a commitment to meeting evolving customer expectations. As e-commerce continues to evolve, businesses will need to adapt, innovate, and navigate the complex challenges of the digital landscape to remain competitive and relevant in the dynamic world of online commerce.

Chapter 4: Affiliate Marketing

Affiliate marketing stands as a dynamic and robust mechanism in the vast landscape of digital commerce. It's a strategic partnership between a merchant or seller and an affiliate or marketer, fostering a symbiotic relationship where both parties reap benefits.

At its core, affiliate marketing operates on a performance-based model. The merchant, often the product or service creator, seeks to expand their reach and sales. On the other hand, the affiliate, acting as an intermediary, promotes the merchant's products or services through various digital channels in exchange for a commission or a predetermined reward for each successful sale or action, such as a click, lead, or sale.

The fundamental structure of affiliate marketing involves three key players: the merchant, the affiliate, and the consumer. The merchant provides the product or service, the affiliate markets it, and the consumer purchases it. This triangular relationship forms the cornerstone of affiliate marketing's success.

The process commences with the merchant developing an affiliate program, establishing terms, conditions, and commission rates. This program outlines the expectations for affiliates, including the payment structure, promotional guidelines, and performance metrics.

Affiliates join these programs by signing up through affiliate networks, which act as intermediaries connecting merchants and affiliates. These networks streamline the process by managing the tracking of sales, ensuring proper commission payouts, and providing a platform for both merchants and affiliates to engage and collaborate.

Affiliate marketers leverage various digital channels to promote products or services, such as websites, blogs, social media platforms, email marketing, video content, and more. Through compelling content, reviews, tutorials, or advertisements, affiliates aim to attract potential consumers, drive traffic to the merchant's site, and ultimately facilitate conversions.

One of the most significant advantages of affiliate marketing is its flexibility and scalability. It allows individuals to delve into entrepreneurship without the need to create products or services from scratch. Affiliates can choose products aligned with their niche, interests, or expertise, making it a highly versatile business model.

Moreover, the financial rewards in affiliate marketing are directly tied to performance. The more effective an affiliate is in driving sales, the higher their earning potential. This performance-based structure incentivizes affiliates to innovate and optimize their marketing strategies continuously.

Affiliate marketing has undergone significant evolution with the advent of technology and digital platforms. Tracking tools and analytics have become more sophisticated, providing detailed insights into consumer behavior, enabling affiliates to refine their marketing strategies and enhance their targeting efforts.

However, despite its myriad advantages, affiliate marketing isn't devoid of challenges. The competitive landscape demands affiliates to stay updated with the latest trends, adapt to changes in algorithms, and continuously refine their strategies to remain relevant in the dynamic digital space. Moreover, building and maintaining trust with an audience is crucial for long-term success.

This model's success depends on the quality and authenticity of the content created by affiliates. Transparency, ethical promotional practices, and genuine recommendations are essential to establish trust with the audience. Building a loyal following involves consistently delivering value, being honest in product reviews, and understanding the audience's needs.

In conclusion, affiliate marketing represents a dynamic and lucrative avenue in the digital marketing sphere. Its structure fosters mutually beneficial relationships between merchants, affiliates, and consumers. The key to success lies in the ability of affiliates to create valuable, compelling content, build trust, and adapt to the ever-evolving digital landscape. As technology continues to advance, affiliate marketing will likely evolve further, offering new opportunities and challenges for those engaged in this dynamic field.

Chapter 5: Blogging for Revenue

Blogging for revenue has become a popular and potentially lucrative venture in the digital age. It's a creative platform that allows individuals to express themselves, share knowledge, and engage with a wide audience while also generating income. While the concept of blogging for profit might seem straightforward, it's a multifaceted journey that involves strategic planning, consistent effort, and various approaches to monetization.

The Initial Steps:

Starting a blog typically begins with identifying your niche or area of expertise. Whether it's travel, fashion, technology, food, personal development, or any other field, selecting a niche that aligns with your interests, knowledge, and the potential audience's demands is crucial. Research and analysis play a vital role in this stage as you aim to find a balance between your passion and a viable market.

Once the niche is established, creating a content strategy becomes the next step. Quality content is the backbone of a successful blog. Generating valuable, engaging, and original content is key to attracting and retaining an audience. This can involve writing articles, creating videos, podcasts, infographics, or a combination of media formats. Maintaining a consistent posting schedule helps in building reader anticipation and loyalty.

Monetization Strategies:

There are numerous ways to monetize a blog:

1. **Advertising:** Displaying ads through platforms like Google AdSense or partnering with companies directly. This involves earning revenue based on pay-per-click or pay-per-impression.

2. **Affiliate Marketing:** Promoting products or services and earning a commission on sales made through unique affiliate links. Building trust with your audience is crucial in this method.

3. **Sponsored Content:** Collaborating with brands to create content (reviews, sponsored posts, etc.) in exchange for payment or products. Transparency and maintaining your authenticity are vital in sponsored content.

4. **Selling Products/Services:** Creating and selling your own products, merchandise, courses, or

services related to your niche. This can include eBooks, online courses, consultancy services, etc.

5. **Membership/Subscriptions:** Offering premium content or exclusive access to a community for a subscription fee.

Challenges and Considerations:

While blogging for revenue can be rewarding, it comes with its own set of challenges:

1. **Consistency and Quality:** Maintaining a consistent posting schedule while ensuring the quality of the content can be demanding. Quality content is crucial for reader engagement and loyalty.

2. **Building an Audience:** Attracting an audience and keeping them engaged requires time and effort. It involves marketing, networking, and possibly utilizing social media to grow your reach.

3. **Monetization Balance:** Finding the right balance between monetization strategies and keeping the content authentic and valuable to your audience is crucial. Too many ads or promotions can alienate readers.

4. **SEO and Analytics:** Understanding Search Engine Optimization (SEO) and analyzing website

metrics is essential for improving visibility and tailoring content based on audience preferences.

Success in the world of blogging often requires a combination of passion, dedication, creativity, adaptability, and a solid understanding of your audience's needs and preferences. It's a dynamic field that continuously evolves, requiring constant learning and adjustment to stay relevant and successful. With the right approach, a well-executed blog has the potential to become a fulfilling source of revenue.

Chapter 6: Content Creation and Monetization

In the ever-evolving landscape of content creation and monetization, the symbiotic relationship between creators and their audience has undergone a remarkable transformation. This narrative journey explores the intricate dance between the art of content creation and the strategic pursuit of monetization in the digital age.

The Genesis of Content Creation

Content creation, once a niche endeavor, has burgeoned into a multi-faceted realm where individuals express themselves through diverse mediums—be it the written word, visual arts, audio-visual presentations, or interactive media. The genesis often emerges from a compelling drive—a passion to communicate, entertain, educate, or provoke thought. It might be a writer crafting compelling stories, a filmmaker creating immersive worlds, a musician composing emotive melodies, or a visual artist painting vibrant canvases.

For creators, the process is a journey of discovery and self-expression. They navigate a creative landscape, aiming to capture emotions, concepts, or stories that resonate with their audience. This journey begins with ideation, the spark of inspiration that fuels the creation process. It involves brainstorming, research, and often a deeply personal connection to the subject matter. Whether it's an article, a video, a podcast, or any form of content, the creator invests their time, energy, and skill into bringing their vision to life.

The Power of Storytelling

At the heart of content creation lies the power of storytelling. Whether overt or subtle, storytelling is the thread that weaves together the fabric of human connection. It captivates the audience, drawing them into the narrative, allowing them to relate, empathize, or escape into another world.

Creators, in their pursuit of audience engagement, harness this power of storytelling. They craft narratives that resonate, connecting emotionally, intellectually, or even spiritually with their audience. From relatable personal anecdotes to grand, imaginative universes, the art of storytelling is a foundational element in successful content creation.

The Digital Revolution

The emergence of the digital age has revolutionized content creation. With the advent of the internet, social media, and digital platforms, creators now have unprecedented access to global audiences. The democratization of content creation tools and platforms has allowed individuals from diverse backgrounds to share their stories, ideas, and creativity.

Digital platforms have become the stage where creators showcase their work. Be it YouTube, Instagram, TikTok, podcasts, blogs, or streaming services like Twitch, these platforms offer a vast audience reach. The instantaneous feedback and engagement from viewers shape the content, influencing its trajectory.

Moreover, the rise of social media has transformed the relationship between creators and their audience. It's no longer a unidirectional flow of content; it's a dynamic, interactive exchange. The audience becomes an integral part of the creative process, offering feedback, suggestions, and becoming an engaged community.

Monetization Strategies

Monetizing content has become an essential aspect for creators seeking sustainability and growth in their craft. Several monetization models exist, each with its own benefits and challenges.

1. **Advertising Revenue:** One of the primary sources of income for many content creators is through advertising. Platforms like YouTube offer monetization through ad revenue sharing, where creators earn based on ad views or clicks. However, this model often requires substantial viewership to generate significant income.

2. **Subscription/Membership:** Some creators opt for subscription-based models. Platforms like Patreon allow creators to offer exclusive content or perks to their paying subscribers. This fosters a sense of community and ensures a more reliable income stream, as the audience directly supports the creator.

3. **Sponsorships and Partnerships:** Collaborating with brands for sponsorships or partnerships is another avenue for monetization. Creators endorse products or services in their content, earning a fee

in return. This method often requires a delicate balance to maintain authenticity while promoting sponsored content.

4. **Merchandise and Product Sales:** Many creators leverage their brand by selling merchandise or creating products aligned with their content. This could include anything from clothing lines to books, digital tools, or even online courses.

5. **Crowdfunding:** Platforms like Kickstarter or Indiegogo enable creators to pitch their projects to the public and secure funding. This method allows creators to finance their endeavors while directly involving their audience in the creation process.

Challenges and Strategies

While the potential for monetization exists, navigating the landscape of content creation and monetization is not without its challenges.

1. **Content Quality and Consistency:** Creating high-quality, consistent content that resonates with the audience is a perpetual challenge. It demands creativity, dedication, and the ability to adapt to changing audience preferences.

2. Monetization Balance: Finding the right balance between monetization and preserving the integrity of the content is crucial. Over-commercialization can alienate the audience, impacting the authenticity and trust built over time.

3. Algorithm Changes and Platform Dynamics: The ever-evolving algorithms of digital platforms can significantly impact a creator's visibility. Understanding and adapting to these changes is essential for maintaining audience engagement.

4. Audience Engagement and Community Building: Nurturing an engaged and supportive audience requires continuous effort. Creators often need to interact with their audience, foster a sense of community, and respond to feedback and comments.

5. Diversification and Sustainability: Relying on a single monetization strategy can be risky. Diversification—across platforms, revenue streams, and content types—can offer a more sustainable approach.

Conclusion

The world of content creation and monetization is a vibrant, challenging, and rewarding landscape. It's a space where creativity, technology, and business converge, offering opportunities for individuals to share their stories and talents with a global audience.

For creators, the journey is multifaceted, involving artistic expression, audience engagement, and the navigation of diverse monetization strategies. The key lies in finding a harmonious balance between creative integrity and sustainable income generation. In this digital age, the fusion of storytelling, technology, and entrepreneurial acumen opens doors to a world where creativity thrives and where creators can carve their paths while inspiring and entertaining audiences worldwide.

Chapter 7: Online Surveys and Market Research

Market research, in its many forms, is an essential tool for businesses to understand their audience, refine their products or services, and adapt to ever-evolving consumer demands. In recent years, online surveys have emerged as a pivotal component of market research due to their accessibility, cost-effectiveness, and ability to reach a wide and diverse audience.

Imagine a bustling metropolis, where businesses strive to understand the intricate needs and desires of the people who populate its streets. Online surveys act as the thoroughfares through which companies navigate this landscape, aiming to gather valuable insights, much like explorers charting uncharted territory.

These surveys are akin to digital questionnaires, designed with precision to extract specific information, opinions, and preferences from participants. Unlike traditional methods that required physical distribution and collection of surveys, the digital realm presents a revolutionary avenue.

46

With just a few clicks, a company can create and distribute surveys to thousands, even millions, across the globe.

The beauty of online surveys lies in their adaptability and reach. They can target a specific demographic, catering questions precisely to the interests and behaviors of a particular group. For instance, a cosmetics company might seek insights from women aged 25-40, living in urban areas, to understand their skincare habits and preferences. By tailoring questions to suit this demographic, the survey becomes a tool to glean highly pertinent data.

Furthermore, these surveys offer a level of anonymity that encourages respondents to provide candid and honest feedback. Participants often feel more comfortable expressing their genuine opinions without the pressures of face-to-face interaction. This anonymity can be crucial for acquiring unfiltered insights, shedding light on nuanced consumer sentiments.

The design of online surveys is an art in itself. Crafting questions that elicit clear, concise, and actionable responses requires careful consideration. Closed-ended queries with multiple-choice options provide quantifiable data, making it easier to analyze and interpret. Open-ended

47

questions, on the other hand, invite participants to elaborate on their thoughts, providing qualitative richness to the findings.

As these surveys land in the inboxes of individuals or pop up on websites, they beckon the participation of the digital populace. Incentives, such as discounts, gift cards, or entry into sweepstakes, often sweeten the deal, encouraging higher response rates. Sometimes, the allure of contributing to the improvement of a product or service is motivation enough for individuals to partake.

Once responses flood in, the real work begins. Analyzing the collected data is akin to sifting through a vast library, sorting and categorizing the information gathered. Sophisticated software often aids in this process, organizing the data into comprehensible graphs, charts, and tables, offering a visual narrative of consumer behaviors, opinions, and preferences.

From a broader perspective, online surveys are just one facet of the expansive field of market research. They play a significant role in shaping the strategies of businesses, guiding decisions that can influence product development, marketing campaigns, and even the very essence of a brand's identity.

However, while these surveys offer a treasure trove of insights, their effectiveness hinges on certain factors. The phrasing of questions must be clear and unbiased, avoiding leading or loaded language that might skew results. Additionally, the size and representativeness of the sample pool are crucial. A small, homogenous group might not accurately reflect the diverse sentiments of the larger population.

Moreover, the ever-evolving digital landscape introduces both opportunities and challenges. With the proliferation of online surveys, the attention span of participants dwindles, leading to survey fatigue. Amidst the deluge of emails and notifications, the quest for genuine responses becomes a challenge in itself. Marketers must devise innovative strategies to capture attention and encourage engagement.

Despite these challenges, online surveys remain a cornerstone of market research, providing a window into the thoughts, desires, and needs of consumers worldwide. Their adaptability, accessibility, and ability to garner substantial data make them an invaluable tool for companies navigating the complex realm of consumer preferences and market trends.

In conclusion, online surveys represent more than a mere collection of data points—they are a conduit for understanding the human experience, decoding the intricate tapestry of consumer behavior, and guiding businesses toward meeting the ever-changing demands of the market. As technology continues to advance and consumer preferences evolve, the role of online surveys in market research will undoubtedly continue to expand and shape the landscape of commerce in the digital age.

Chapter 8: Online Tutoring and Education

Online tutoring and education have undergone a profound transformation in recent years, reshaping the way we learn and access educational resources. The digital age has ushered in a revolution in the field of education, and online tutoring stands as one of its most prominent manifestations. It's a realm that transcends geographical barriers, offering a vast array of educational opportunities to students, professionals, and lifelong learners worldwide.

The evolution of online tutoring and education can be attributed to a confluence of factors. Advancements in technology, particularly the widespread availability of high-speed internet, have played a pivotal role in making remote learning a feasible and effective alternative to traditional in-person education. This technological advancement has made it possible for students to access educational resources, interact with tutors, and participate in virtual classrooms from the comfort of their homes.

The convenience and flexibility of online tutoring are among its most compelling advantages. Learners now have the freedom to schedule their study sessions at their convenience, removing the constraints of fixed timetables. This flexibility is especially beneficial for working professionals, parents, or individuals with busy schedules, as it allows them to pursue education without compromising their other responsibilities.

Moreover, online tutoring caters to diverse learning styles and preferences. The availability of various multimedia resources, interactive tools, and adaptive learning platforms allows for personalized and self-paced learning experiences. These resources can be tailored to suit individual needs, ensuring that students can learn at their own speed and in their preferred manner, whether through visual, auditory, or kinesthetic methods.

One of the most significant boons of online tutoring is its global reach. Geographical boundaries no longer limit access to education. Students can connect with tutors and educational institutions from different parts of the world, gaining exposure to diverse perspectives, teaching styles, and cultural experiences. This exchange enriches the learning process, fostering a global mindset and understanding.

The interactive nature of online tutoring platforms contributes to a dynamic learning environment. Students can engage in real-time discussions, collaborative group projects, and receive instant feedback from instructors or peers. These interactions simulate the feel of a traditional classroom, albeit in a virtual setting, fostering a sense of community and encouraging active participation.

The rise of Artificial Intelligence (AI) and machine learning has further enhanced the online tutoring experience. AI-powered tools can analyze a student's learning patterns and customize learning materials to match their strengths and areas that need improvement. This adaptive learning approach ensures a more targeted and efficient learning process, ultimately leading to better educational outcomes.

Despite these advantages, online tutoring also presents its own set of challenges. The lack of physical presence and face-to-face interaction can sometimes create a sense of disconnect or isolation. For some learners, the absence of in-person guidance and immediate assistance may pose a hurdle in the learning process. Additionally, technical issues, such as unstable internet connections or unfamiliarity with online platforms, can impede the learning experience.

Another concern associated with online tutoring is the issue of credibility and quality. The internet is flooded with a myriad of educational resources, and not all may adhere to rigorous academic standards. Therefore, ensuring the credibility and reliability of online educational materials and tutors becomes crucial.

Furthermore, the digital divide remains a significant obstacle, particularly in areas where access to high-speed internet or necessary technological resources is limited. This inequity in access to online education can exacerbate existing disparities in educational opportunities among various socio-economic groups.

The future of online tutoring and education appears promising, continually evolving to address these challenges and further capitalize on its strengths. As technology continues to advance, the integration of virtual reality, augmented reality, and other innovative tools could revolutionize the learning experience, creating more immersive and interactive educational environments.

In conclusion, online tutoring and education have fundamentally altered the educational landscape, offering unparalleled access, flexibility, and adaptability. While facing certain challenges, its potential to democratize education and cater to diverse learning needs is undeniable. With continuous innovation and adaptation, online tutoring stands poised to continue reshaping and enhancing the way we learn and acquire knowledge in the years to come.

Chapter 9: Virtual Assistance and Remote Work

Virtual assistance and remote work have become integral components of modern work culture, driven by technological advancements, evolving work models, and a changing global landscape. This shift has transformed the traditional notions of employment, introducing new dynamics in how people work, collaborate, and conduct business.

The concept of virtual assistance encompasses a broad spectrum of roles and tasks. Virtual assistants (Vas) are individuals who provide professional, administrative, technical, or creative assistance to clients remotely. This form of work has gained significant traction due to its flexibility, cost-effectiveness, and the convenience it offers both businesses and freelancers. Vas operate from various locations, leveraging technology to communicate, collaborate, and execute tasks without the need for physical presence in an office.

Remote work, closely associated with virtual assistance, extends beyond administrative support to encompass a wide array of professions and industries. This shift towards remote work has been accelerated by several factors. Technological advancements, such as high-speed internet, cloud computing, project management tools, and communication platforms, have significantly contributed to the feasibility and efficiency of remote work.

The benefits of virtual assistance and remote work are numerous. For individuals, the flexibility to work from any location and the ability to manage their own schedules can enhance work-life balance. This flexibility is particularly attractive to parents, caregivers, digital nomads, and individuals seeking more control over their time and lifestyle.

From an organizational perspective, remote work allows companies to tap into a global talent pool, reducing overhead costs associated with maintaining physical office spaces. It fosters diversity and inclusivity by enabling individuals from different geographical locations and backgrounds to collaborate and contribute their unique perspectives.

However, this shift is not without challenges. One of the primary concerns is the potential impact on team dynamics and collaboration. Without face-to-face interactions, building rapport, fostering a strong team culture, and effective communication can become challenging. Additionally, ensuring data security and maintaining productivity across different time zones and cultures requires careful planning and implementation of robust systems and procedures.

The COVID-19 pandemic further accelerated the adoption of remote work. Many organizations were forced to transition to remote setups almost overnight, which prompted a reevaluation of traditional work structures. Companies that had been hesitant to embrace remote work were compelled to do so, and this period served as a litmus test, demonstrating that remote work could be successful, productive, and sustainable.

The future of work seems to be increasingly intertwined with virtual assistance and remote work. As technology continues to advance, it is expected that more professions will adapt to remote models, offering flexibility to employees and redefining the traditional concepts of workspaces. The hybrid model, blending remote and in-person work, might become the norm, allowing individuals and organizations to leverage the best of both worlds.

In conclusion, virtual assistance and remote work have revolutionized the way we perceive and execute work. They offer unparalleled flexibility, a broader talent pool, and significant cost savings for both individuals and organizations. While challenges exist, with careful management and the right tools and strategies in place, remote work stands as a powerful and sustainable model that will continue to shape the future of work.

Chapter 10: Cryptocurrency and Online Trading

Cryptocurrency and online trading represent two intertwined aspects of the modern financial landscape that have significantly altered the way we perceive, handle, and invest in assets. Their emergence and convergence have reshaped traditional financial systems, empowering individuals worldwide to participate in the global economy in unprecedented ways.

The inception of cryptocurrencies, notably marked by the introduction of Bitcoin in 2009 by the pseudonymous creator Satoshi Nakamoto, introduced a revolutionary decentralized digital currency. Unlike traditional currencies issued and regulated by central authorities, cryptocurrencies operate on a decentralized ledger technology called blockchain. This decentralized nature, powered by cryptography, offers security, transparency, and, to a large extent, anonymity.

The surge of cryptocurrencies brought forth an entirely new market for investors, speculators, and technology enthusiasts. The remarkable rise in the value of Bitcoin and other altcoins led to both fervor and skepticism. Bitcoin's meteoric rise, from mere cents to thousands of dollars, captured the attention of mainstream media and traditional financial institutions. This upward trajectory wasn't without volatility, marked by dramatic price swings that attracted both fervent supporters and cautious onlookers.

Simultaneously, online trading platforms emerged as gateways for individuals to participate in this burgeoning digital asset market. These platforms, such as Coinbase, Binance, and Kraken, allowed users to buy, sell, and trade cryptocurrencies, simplifying the process through user-friendly interfaces. Their ease of use, coupled with low entry barriers, facilitated widespread adoption.

The allure of cryptocurrency investment and online trading lies in their accessibility and the potential for significant financial gains. These digital currencies are traded 24/7, providing a borderless financial ecosystem. Additionally, the ability to buy fractional shares of cryptocurrencies, facilitating smaller investments, has made them accessible to a broad spectrum of investors.

However, with the potential for high returns come inherent risks. The cryptocurrency market is highly volatile, subject to sudden and substantial price fluctuations. Its speculative nature often results in investors experiencing both significant gains and staggering losses within short time frames. Regulatory uncertainties, security concerns, and susceptibility to market manipulation further amplify the risks associated with cryptocurrency investment.

The convergence of cryptocurrency and online trading has led to an evolving financial landscape, challenging conventional norms and fostering debates on its implications. On one hand, proponents tout the democratization of finance, envisioning a future where individuals have greater control over their assets without intermediaries. They highlight the potential for financial inclusion, particularly in regions with limited access to traditional banking services.

Conversely, critics caution against the unregulated nature of cryptocurrencies, citing concerns over potential illicit activities like money laundering, fraud, and the lack of investor protections. The absence of a central authority overseeing these digital assets raises questions about accountability and stability in the event of a market crash or unforeseen circumstances.

Moreover, the intersection of cryptocurrency and online trading has brought attention to the broader discussion of the future of money and the financial system. Governments and regulatory bodies are grappling with how to integrate and regulate cryptocurrencies within existing frameworks. The push and pull between embracing innovation and ensuring consumer protection continues to shape policies around the world.

In conclusion, the emergence and convergence of cryptocurrency and online trading represent a paradigm shift in the financial landscape. It has empowered individuals to engage in a decentralized, global economy with unprecedented opportunities and risks. As these technologies continue to evolve, the future of finance is likely to be influenced by the ongoing dialogue between innovation, regulation, and the pursuit of financial inclusivity.

Chapter 11: Building and Monetizing a Social Media Presence

Building and monetizing a social media presence is a multifaceted journey that involves dedication, strategy, and a deep understanding of both your audience and the platform you're using. It's a fascinating realm where creativity, consistency, and community engagement play pivotal roles in establishing a successful presence.

1. Establishing Your Presence

To embark on this journey, the initial step is to determine your niche. Whether it's lifestyle, fashion, technology, travel, or any other category, finding your niche is crucial. This specialization helps in creating content that resonates with a specific audience. Once your niche is defined, it's time to create high-quality, engaging content. Consistency is key here – regular posts or updates maintain visibility and help build a dedicated following. Content could be in various formats such as images, videos, blogs, or a mix of these.

Moreover, optimizing your profile on various social media platforms is crucial. A well-crafted and complete profile with a recognizable profile picture, a captivating bio, and relevant keywords is essential for visibility and discoverability. Hashtags are powerful tools to expand your reach, but they must be used strategically and sparingly.

2. Engagement and Community Building

Engagement is the heart of social media. Interacting with your audience is pivotal – responding to comments, messages, and participating in discussions. This humanizes your brand and creates a strong community. Collaborations with other influencers or brands can significantly expand your reach and expose your content to a wider audience.

3. Monetization Strategies

Once a substantial following and engagement are established, numerous opportunities for monetization become available. These opportunities include:

- **Brand Collaborations and Sponsored Content:** Brands are always on the lookout for influencers to promote their products or services. When your social media presence is strong and engaging, companies may approach you for sponsored content. This can range from a single post to long-term partnerships.

- **Affiliate Marketing:** Promoting products and earning a commission for every sale made through your unique affiliate link can be a lucrative revenue stream. When done transparently and authentically, this can enhance both your credibility and income.

- **Selling Your Own Products or Services:** If you have your products or offer services, social media can serve as an excellent platform to showcase and sell them. Whether it's merchandise, online courses, e-books, or consulting services, your engaged audience can be potential customers.

- **Ad Revenue:** Platforms like YouTube and some other social media networks offer creators the opportunity to earn ad revenue through their content. As your following grows, so does the potential income from advertisements displayed alongside your content.

- **Membership and Subscription Services:** Offering exclusive content or perks to subscribers or members can be a sustainable income stream. Platforms like Patreon, Substack, or even offering exclusive content on platforms like Instagram or Facebook can be a means to monetize your dedicated followers.

- **Selling Rights to Your Content:** If your content is unique or particularly engaging, you may consider licensing its use to other entities, such as media organizations, websites, or other platforms.

4. **Challenges and Consistency**

While the path to monetizing a social media presence is promising, it's important to acknowledge the challenges. The landscape is highly competitive, and success often requires time, patience, and continuous effort. Algorithms change, trends evolve, and the digital sphere is dynamic. To succeed, adaptability and the willingness to learn and evolve are key.

Consistency in content creation and engagement is paramount. It's essential to stay relevant and continuously offer value to your audience. Moreover, being authentic and genuine in your interactions and content is what sets you apart in a space often saturated with inauthenticity.

In conclusion, building and monetizing a social media presence is an exciting yet demanding journey. With the right strategy, dedication, and genuine engagement, it's possible to create not just a following but a thriving business. The combination of finding your niche, engaging your audience, and exploring diverse monetization strategies will pave the way for success in the ever-evolving landscape of social media.

Chapter 12: Creating and Selling Digital Products

Creating and selling digital products has evolved into a thriving industry, driven by the technological advancements and changing consumer preferences of the modern era. This industry encompasses a vast array of digital goods, from e-books, online courses, software, music, graphics, templates, and much more. The allure of digital products lies in their accessibility, scalability, and the ability to cater to niche markets, making it an attractive avenue for entrepreneurs, creators, and businesses alike.

1. The Creative Process:

Creating digital products often begins with a spark of inspiration or identifying a gap in the market. Whether it's a writer crafting an e-book, a graphic designer developing templates, or a software engineer conceptualizing an app, the process typically involves creativity, expertise, and problem-solving skills.

2. Ideation and Research:

In the initial phase, creators conduct thorough research to understand their target audience, market trends, and potential competitors. This step is crucial as it lays the foundation for a successful digital product. Understanding the needs and preferences of the audience helps in shaping the product idea and its features.

3. Development and Design:

Once the concept is clear, creators move on to the development and design phase. This might involve writing, designing, coding, or other forms of content creation. It's a meticulous process that requires attention to detail, creativity, and technical skills.

4. Testing and Refinement:

Before launching the product, testing and refinement play a significant role. Creators often seek feedback from beta users or conduct usability tests to identify and rectify any potential issues. This iterative process ensures a polished final product that meets the audience's needs.

5. Platforms and Distribution:

Selling digital products involves choosing the right platforms for distribution and sales. Online marketplaces, personal websites, and specialized platforms serve as avenues for reaching customers. Each platform offers its own set of advantages and considerations.

6. Online Marketplaces:

Platforms like Amazon, Etsy, or platforms like Udemy for courses provide vast visibility to creators due to their large user base. However, they may also charge fees and have certain limitations on branding and marketing.

7. Personal Websites:

Setting up an independent website or using services like Shopify allows creators to have more control over branding, pricing, and customer relationships. This approach demands a robust marketing strategy to drive traffic to the site.

8. Specialized Platforms:

For niche products, specialized platforms often cater to specific audiences. For instance, if you're selling digital art, platforms like Society6 or Redbubble might be suitable.

9. Marketing and Sales:

The success of digital products heavily relies on marketing strategies. With the vast array of products available online, standing out and reaching the target audience is a crucial challenge.

10. Content Marketing:

Creating valuable content related to the digital product, such as blog posts, videos, or social media content, helps in attracting and engaging potential customers. Content should be informative, entertaining, and showcase the value of the product.

11. SEO and Keywords:

Search Engine Optimization (SEO) plays a pivotal role in making the product discoverable. Understanding keywords and optimizing product descriptions, titles, and content can enhance visibility on search engines.

12. Social Media and Influencers:

Utilizing social media platforms and collaborating with influencers in the respective niche can significantly expand the product's reach. Social media presence and endorsements can build credibility and attract potential customers.

13. Customer Engagement and Support:

Once the product is in the market, customer engagement and support are crucial for building a loyal customer base.

14. Customer Service:

Prompt and effective customer service helps in retaining customers and building trust. Timely responses to queries and concerns contribute to a positive customer experience.

15. Feedback and Iteration:

Constantly seeking feedback from customers allows creators to improve their products. Iterating based on customer suggestions or market changes keeps the product relevant and competitive.

16. Legal and Security Aspects:

When selling digital products, creators need to consider legal and security aspects to protect their work and customers.

17. Copyright and Intellectual Property:

Understanding copyright laws and protecting intellectual property rights is essential to prevent plagiarism and ensure the creator's work is safeguarded.

18. Security and Privacy:

Ensuring secure transactions and safeguarding customer data is imperative. Using secure payment gateways and implementing data protection measures is crucial for maintaining trust.

In conclusion, the process of creating and selling digital products involves a blend of creativity, market understanding, strategic planning, and continuous adaptation. The digital marketplace offers vast opportunities for creators to share their expertise, entertain, educate, and meet the evolving needs of consumers worldwide. Success in this space often comes from a combination of a quality product, effective marketing, customer engagement, and a keen eye on industry trends.

Chapter 13: Print on Demand and Merchandise Sales

Print on Demand (POD) and merchandise sales represent a significant shift in how products are created, marketed, and sold in today's digital landscape. This innovative business model has transformed the way artists, creators, and entrepreneurs bring their designs and products to the market without the need for upfront inventory or substantial investment. The concept of print on demand involves creating custom-designed products that are manufactured and shipped only when an order is placed, eliminating the need for holding inventory or dealing with excess stock.

The rise of print on demand services has been fueled by technological advancements and the accessibility of e-commerce platforms, allowing individuals to create and sell their unique designs or artwork on various merchandise, ranging from t-shirts, mugs, phone cases, posters, and more. This method empowers artists and designers to turn their creativity into tangible products without the burden of managing production, fulfillment, or inventory.

Merchandise sales, in the context of print on demand, cover a broad spectrum of items that can be customized and sold. It's not just about the product itself but the design or artwork that's printed on it. Artists, illustrators, and graphic designers often leverage POD services to showcase their art on different products, enabling them to reach a broader audience and monetize their creativity.

The process typically begins with an artist or designer creating a design. This could be an original illustration, a catchy phrase, a digital artwork, or any form of creative content. Once the design is ready, it's uploaded to a print on demand platform. These platforms offer a range of products that can be customized, and the artist can choose the items they want to sell their designs on.

Customers then discover these designs either through the platform itself or through marketing efforts by the creators. When a customer places an order for a product featuring a specific design, the print on demand service takes care of the manufacturing, printing the design on the chosen merchandise, packaging, and shipping it directly to the customer. The artist receives a portion of the sales as their profit, while the print on demand service earns from the production costs and platform fees.

One of the significant advantages of print on demand is its low barrier to entry. It allows creators to start selling their designs with minimal upfront costs. This democratization of product creation has led to an explosion of creativity and a diverse array of products in the market.

Moreover, print on demand also provides scalability. As the designs gain popularity and attract a larger audience, creators can leverage the platform's infrastructure to handle the increased demand without worrying about production constraints or logistics. This scalability allows for a broader reach and potential for increased earnings.

The success of print on demand and merchandise sales heavily relies on effective marketing and the creator's ability to stand out in a competitive market. With numerous creators vying for attention, establishing a unique brand and effective marketing strategy becomes crucial. Social media, influencer partnerships, SEO optimization, and targeted advertising are some of the strategies used to reach potential customers and drive sales.

The future of print on demand and merchandise sales seems promising. As technology continues to advance, providing better printing techniques, superior quality products, and faster delivery times, the potential for growth in this sector is significant. Additionally, as consumer preferences evolve, the demand for custom, unique, and personalized products is expected to continue growing, further fueling the expansion of print on demand and merchandise sales.

However, challenges exist within this industry. As the market becomes more saturated, the need for original, high-quality designs becomes more critical. Additionally, there might be concerns regarding intellectual property rights, copyright issues, and the need for creators to stand out amidst the competition.

In conclusion, print on demand and merchandise sales have revolutionized the way artists, designers, and entrepreneurs bring their creations to the market. It has democratized the process, allowing individuals to turn their creativity into a source of income without the traditional constraints of production, inventory, and distribution. As technology and consumer preferences continue to evolve, this industry is poised for further growth and innovation, offering endless opportunities for creators to showcase their work and for consumers to access unique, personalized products.

Chapter 14: Gaming and eSports Earnings

The world of gaming and eSports has undergone a remarkable evolution in recent years, transforming from a mere pastime into a booming industry. Within this realm, earnings have skyrocketed, reflecting the growing interest, dedication, and investment in these fields. The amalgamation of technological advancements, changing consumer habits, and the allure of competitive gaming has laid the foundation for considerable earnings across various sectors.

The revenue streams in gaming and eSports are multifaceted. From professional gamers to game developers, event organizers, sponsors, and streaming platforms, the avenues through which earnings are generated are diverse and expanding.

Professional gamers, once regarded as enthusiasts indulging in a niche hobby, now command substantial earnings. Competitive gaming, with its range of tournaments and leagues, has turned professional gamers into high-earning individuals. These gamers, often displaying unparalleled skills in popular games like Dota 2, League of Legends, CS:GO, and Fortnite, can secure significant prize money from competitions and endorsements from gaming brands seeking to leverage their influence. The most successful players often boast earnings in the millions, with some even becoming internationally recognized celebrities.

Moreover, streaming platforms such as Twitch and YouTube have redefined the relationship between gamers and their audience. Through live broadcasts and recorded content, these platforms enable gamers to build a following and monetize their content through subscriptions, donations, and sponsorships. Successful streamers can accumulate substantial earnings through these channels, with some of the top streamers amassing substantial wealth through their engaging content and loyal fan base.

The business of game development itself is a major revenue-generating sector. Game developers, whether independent or part of larger studios, earn revenue through the sale of games, downloadable content, and in-game purchases. The industry's creativity and innovation continue to draw in consumers, resulting in significant profits for successful game developers.

Furthermore, eSports events and tournaments have become colossal spectacles, drawing in millions of viewers worldwide. These events, featuring professional teams battling it out in high-stakes competitions, attract sponsorship deals, ticket sales, and advertising revenue. The prize pools for major tournaments have seen dramatic increases, with some competitions offering millions of dollars in winnings.

Sponsorship and advertising play a vital role in the gaming and eSports industry's financial landscape. Companies seeking to tap into the vast gaming audience often partner with players, teams, and events to promote their products. The appeal of reaching a highly engaged and tech-savvy demographic has led to significant investments from various industries, further driving the revenue within gaming and eSports.

The gaming and eSports industry's earnings are not just limited to the aforementioned sectors. It extends to merchandise sales, licensing deals, media rights, and more. The continual growth of this industry has resulted in a vibrant ecosystem, where various stakeholders contribute to its financial success.

This incredible surge in earnings within the gaming and eSports domains showcases not only the immense popularity and profitability but also the promising future of an industry that has firmly established itself as a major player in the global entertainment and economic landscape. As technology advances and the audience's enthusiasm continues to expand, the prospects for increased earnings in gaming and eSports appear boundless.

Chapter 15: Stock Photography and Art Sales

T he world of stock photography and art sales is a multifaceted industry that bridges the gap between artistic expression and commercial viability. It's a realm where creativity intersects with commerce, offering both artists and buyers a platform to exchange visual content for various purposes. The landscape of stock photography and art sales has evolved significantly over the years, shaped by technological advancements, changing consumer demands, and the democratization of content creation.

1. The Evolution of Stock Photography and Art Sales

The concept of stock photography dates back to the early 20th century when agencies began amassing collections of images for commercial purposes. These collections comprised photographs and illustrations used by advertisers, publishers, and businesses. However, it was in the digital age that the industry saw a significant transformation. The advent of the internet, digital cameras, and online platforms revolutionized the way images were created, stored, and distributed.

Online marketplaces and platforms emerged, providing a space for photographers, artists, and creators to upload and sell their work. Companies like Shutterstock, Adobe Stock, Getty Images, and others revolutionized the industry, creating vast repositories of visual content accessible to buyers worldwide.

2. The Role of Stock Photography in Modern Society

Stock photography has become an integral part of modern communication. It caters to a wide range of industries, including advertising, publishing, web design, social media, and more. Businesses often turn to stock photography for their marketing campaigns, as it offers a cost-effective and convenient solution for obtaining high-quality images. It allows them to access a vast array of visual content without the expenses associated with commissioned photoshoots or exclusive licensing.

The impact of stock photography extends beyond the commercial sphere. It has influenced cultural narratives, representing and reflecting societal trends, diversity, and global perspectives. Stock images shape our visual language, influencing how we perceive and communicate ideas, emotions, and stories.

3.   Challenges and Opportunities in the Industry

While the stock photography and art sales industry offer tremendous opportunities, it's not without its challenges. One of the primary challenges is the balance between artistic integrity and commercial appeal. Artists often face the dilemma of creating work that is both creatively fulfilling and commercially viable. Balancing these two aspects is crucial in a competitive market.

Another challenge is standing out in a crowded space. With the proliferation of digital content, it can be difficult for individual artists to gain visibility and recognition. Success often depends on the ability to create unique, high-quality content and effectively market it to the right audience.

However, amidst these challenges lie numerous opportunities. The industry's growth offers a chance for artists to showcase their work on a global scale. The ease of digital platforms allows creators to reach a vast audience and diversify their revenue streams. Furthermore, the demand for authentic, diverse, and high-quality visual content continues to increase, presenting an opportunity for artists to cater to these needs.

4. Trends and Future of Stock Photography and Art Sales

Several trends are shaping the future of the industry. Personalization and authenticity are becoming increasingly important. Buyers seek images that reflect real-life situations, diversity, and authenticity. As a result, there is a growing demand for genuine, candid, and relatable visuals that connect with audiences on a deeper level.

Technology, particularly artificial intelligence and machine learning, is also influencing the industry. These technologies aid in content curation, search optimization, and even image creation. They assist in matching the right content with the right audience, streamlining the process for both buyers and sellers.

Moreover, the rise of mobile photography has democratized the creation of visual content. Smartphones equipped with high-quality cameras have enabled anyone to become a content creator. This trend has led to an explosion of user-generated content, adding to the vast pool of available images.

As for the future, the industry is expected to continue evolving. Innovation in technology, changing consumer behaviors, and the need for diverse and inclusive visuals will likely drive the direction of stock photography and art sales. Artists and creators will need to adapt to these changes, embrace new technologies, and continue to produce compelling and relevant content to thrive in this dynamic landscape.

5. Conclusion

Stock photography and art sales represent a dynamic fusion of artistry and commerce. The industry has evolved significantly, driven by technological advancements and changing consumer demands. It plays a crucial role in modern communication, catering to a wide array of industries and influencing cultural narratives.

The challenges in the industry are met with ample opportunities for artists and creators. Success hinges on striking a balance between creative integrity and commercial appeal while adapting to emerging trends and technologies. The future of stock photography and art sales looks promising, with a continued focus on authenticity, diversity, and the integration of cutting-edge technologies. Ultimately, the industry will continue to thrive as it adapts to the ever-changing landscape of visual content creation and distribution.

Chapter 16: Web Development and Design Opportunities

Web development and design are two intertwined disciplines that offer a multitude of opportunities and possibilities. In today's digital age, the internet serves as a cornerstone for communication, commerce, and information dissemination. Web development involves the creation and maintenance of websites and web applications, focusing on both the technical and functional aspects. On the other hand, web design concentrates on the aesthetic and user experience elements, including layout, visual appeal, and usability.

The opportunities within this field are vast and continually expanding. With the surge in e-commerce, online services, and the digital transformation of traditional businesses, the demand for web developers and designers is ever-increasing. Whether it's designing a responsive and engaging website, developing complex web applications, or creating user-friendly interfaces, the need for skilled professionals in these areas remains high.

For developers, mastering programming languages and frameworks such as HTML, CSS, JavaScript, Python, Ruby, PHP, and various content management systems like WordPress or Drupal can open doors to various roles in the industry. Full-stack development, front-end, back-end, and specialized areas like cybersecurity or e-commerce development provide diverse paths to explore.

Meanwhile, web designers focus on creating visually compelling and user-friendly interfaces. They work with tools like Adobe Creative Suite, Figma, Sketch, or other design software to craft layouts, typography, color schemes, and visual elements that enhance user experience. Understanding user behavior and creating intuitive, aesthetically pleasing designs is a fundamental aspect of the role.

Moreover, the rise of mobile technologies has created additional opportunities in responsive and mobile web design and development. With the proliferation of smartphones and tablets, ensuring a seamless user experience across various devices has become paramount.

Freelancing and remote work opportunities are also prevalent in this field, allowing professionals to work independently or for various companies, regardless of their geographical location. The gig economy has significantly expanded opportunities for web developers and designers to work on diverse projects for different clients or companies, providing flexibility and autonomy.

Furthermore, the field is constantly evolving. Technologies, frameworks, and trends change rapidly, creating a continuous need for professionals to stay updated with the latest tools and best practices. This dynamic nature of the industry offers ongoing opportunities for growth, learning, and innovation.

Lastly, the crossover between web development and emerging technologies like artificial intelligence, augmented reality, and virtual reality presents an exciting frontier for professionals to explore. Integrating these technologies into web development and design can lead to the creation of innovative, immersive, and interactive web experiences.

In conclusion, the world of web development and design offers a myriad of opportunities for individuals with the passion and skills to create, innovate, and adapt in a rapidly evolving digital landscape. Whether in traditional job roles, freelance settings, or pushing the boundaries with cutting-edge technologies, this field is dynamic, constantly evolving, and filled with possibilities for those willing to explore and embrace its ever-changing nature.

Chapter 17: Mobile Apps and Development

In the vast landscape of modern technology, mobile applications stand as the driving force behind a significant transformation in how we interact, work, and engage with the digital world. The concept of mobile applications emerged with the birth of smartphones, which quickly evolved from mere communication devices into powerful, handheld computers. The shift in consumer behavior, driven by the convenience and accessibility of these devices, sparked a revolution in the way we access information and services.

Mobile app development is a multidimensional process that encapsulates creativity, innovation, and technical prowess. It's not just about coding and design; it's an intricate fusion of user experience, functionality, and aesthetic appeal. To create a successful mobile app, developers must navigate through a complex web of considerations, ranging from understanding user needs to utilizing the latest technologies.

The development journey typically begins with an idea or a problem that needs a solution. This seed of an idea is then nurtured through extensive research and conceptualization. Understanding the target audience, their behaviors, and preferences is crucial. It's not just about identifying the problem but also comprehending how the app can seamlessly integrate into users' lives.

Once the concept is fleshed out, the development team delves into the intricacies of app architecture and design. The choice of technology stack, platform (iOS, Android, or both), and the development approach (native, hybrid, or cross-platform) all play pivotal roles in shaping the app's foundation. The user interface (UI) and user experience (UX) design are crafted to ensure an intuitive and engaging environment for the end-users.

Behind the scenes, the development process involves the implementation of various functionalities. This stage requires meticulous coding, thorough testing, and continuous optimization. With the adoption of agile methodologies, developers iteratively build and refine the app, integrating feedback and improvements along the way.

Security, another paramount concern, is woven into the development fabric. As the app will handle sensitive user data, robust security measures must be implemented to safeguard against potential threats and vulnerabilities.

Furthermore, the app development process extends beyond coding and design. Monetization strategies, such as in-app purchases, subscriptions, or advertisements, need to be considered. Also, a comprehensive go-to-market strategy is essential for launching the app successfully, which includes app store optimization, marketing, and user acquisition plans.

The mobile app development landscape is a continuously evolving ecosystem. The constant advancements in technology and changing user expectations necessitate developers to stay abreast of the latest trends and innovations. Emerging technologies like augmented reality (AR), virtual reality (VR), artificial intelligence (AI), and the Internet of Things (IoT) are reshaping the future of mobile applications, offering exciting new possibilities and functionalities.

Moreover, user feedback and post-launch analytics are crucial components in the development process. Understanding how users interact with the app, their pain points, and preferences helps in implementing updates and features that enhance the overall user experience.

In essence, mobile app development is a dynamic and intricate process that involves a harmonious blend of creativity, technology, and user-centric design. The journey from ideation to deployment is filled with challenges, learning experiences, and the thrill of creating something that has the potential to impact the lives of millions worldwide. The continuous evolution of this field ensures that the world of mobile apps will keep surprising and captivating us with innovative solutions and experiences.

Chapter 18: Podcasting for Profit

The realm of podcasting has evolved from a niche hobby to a powerful and lucrative industry. As the digital landscape continues to expand, podcasting for profit has emerged as a viable avenue for content creators, entrepreneurs, and businesses alike. The appeal of podcasting lies in its versatility, allowing individuals to explore diverse topics, share stories, and connect with audiences on a personal level. But with the growing number of podcasts, standing out and generating revenue requires a strategic approach.

Creating a successful podcast involves a multi-faceted strategy that encompasses content creation, audience engagement, marketing, monetization, and more. Below, we delve into the various aspects of podcasting for profit.

1. Content Creation:

At the core of a successful podcast is compelling content. Identifying a niche or topic that resonates with an audience is crucial. Your content should be engaging, informative, and unique. It could be focused on storytelling, interviews, educational material, discussions, or a combination of these.

Crafting an effective content strategy involves thorough research. Understand your target audience's interests and needs. What topics are they passionate about? What problems can your podcast help solve? Research trends and current events within your niche to keep the content relevant and engaging.

Consistency is key. Maintaining a regular release schedule helps build anticipation and loyalty among your listeners. Whether it's weekly, bi-weekly, or monthly, having a predictable schedule can significantly impact your podcast's success.

2. Quality Production:

Technical quality plays a vital role in retaining and attracting an audience. Invest in good recording equipment, editing software, and a quiet, well-equipped space for recording. Listeners appreciate clear audio, so ensure your production values are high.

3. Audience Engagement:

Building a strong community around your podcast is essential. Engage with your audience through social media, email newsletters, live Q&A sessions, or even creating a dedicated forum for discussion. Interacting with your listeners can foster a sense of belonging and loyalty, leading to a more committed and supportive audience base.

Encourage feedback and listener participation. Ask for reviews, comments, and suggestions for future episodes. This engagement not only strengthens your connection with the audience but also provides valuable insights for improvement.

4. Marketing and Promotion:

To stand out in the sea of podcasts, effective marketing and promotion are crucial. Leverage social media platforms, create compelling teaser clips or trailers, collaborate with other podcasters, and explore guest appearances on other shows to expand your reach.

Utilize SEO strategies by incorporating relevant keywords in your podcast title, description, and episode titles. This helps in better visibility within podcast directories and search engines.

5. Monetization:

Monetization strategies vary and can be implemented individually or in combination. Some common methods include:

- **Advertising and Sponsorships:** Partnering with brands or companies relevant to your niche can bring in revenue through paid sponsorships and advertisements. Advertisers are often attracted to podcasts with a sizable and engaged audience.
- **Crowdfunding and Donations:** Platforms like Patreon or direct donations via PayPal or other methods can help monetize your podcast. Offering exclusive content or perks to donors can incentivize listeners to support your work financially.
- **Merchandise and Products:** Creating and selling branded merchandise, products, or courses related to your podcast's theme can be a source of revenue.
- **Premium Content or Subscriptions:** Offering additional content or early access to episodes for a subscription fee can be an effective monetization model.

6. Legal and Business Considerations:

As your podcast grows, consider the legal and business aspects. Protect your content through copyrights and trademarks where applicable. Consider forming a business entity for your podcast, which can help with liability protection and tax advantages.

Ensure you comply with any regulations related to the content you're producing, especially if your podcast covers sensitive topics or industries.

7. Challenges and Persistence:

Podcasting for profit requires dedication and patience. It's not an overnight success story. Many podcasters face challenges such as finding their audience, maintaining consistency, and coping with the fluctuations in revenue.

However, persistence and adaptability are key. Being open to evolving your content, strategies, and embracing new opportunities or changes in the podcasting landscape can lead to sustained growth and success.

8. Conclusion:

Podcasting for profit is a multifaceted endeavor that requires a combination of quality content, audience engagement, marketing, and monetization strategies. Success in this space often comes from a balance between creativity, dedication, adaptability, and business acumen. As the podcasting landscape continues to evolve, those who are willing to put in the effort, engage with their audience, and continually improve their craft stand a greater chance of reaping the rewards both personally and financially from their podcasting endeavors.

Chapter 19: Remote Services and Consulting

Remote services and consulting have rapidly transformed the way businesses and professionals operate, connect, and thrive in today's interconnected world. With the advent of advanced technology and the evolution of digital communication, the concept of providing services and consultancy remotely has seen an unprecedented surge in popularity and necessity.

The shift to remote services and consulting has been significantly accelerated by the global events of recent years, particularly the COVID-19 pandemic, which forced individuals and businesses to adapt quickly to remote work environments. This paradigm shift has highlighted the importance and feasibility of conducting consultations, delivering services, and offering expertise without the need for physical proximity.

One of the key advantages of remote services and consulting is the accessibility it offers. Geographical barriers are virtually eliminated, allowing professionals to connect with clients, customers, or businesses from across the globe.

This accessibility has broadened the reach of services and consultancy, enabling experts to transcend borders and time zones, facilitating a more globalized approach to problem-solving and expertise sharing.

Moreover, the use of remote services and consulting has not only proven to be efficient but has also shown significant cost-saving benefits. By removing the need for physical office space, commuting, and other associated expenses, both service providers and clients can often reduce their operational costs. This economic advantage has made remote consultancy an attractive option for businesses looking to optimize their budgets without compromising on the quality of expertise they receive.

The adoption of remote services and consulting has been especially prominent in certain sectors. Technology-related services, such as software development, IT support, and digital marketing, have seamlessly adapted to remote models due to their inherently digital nature. However, fields such as education, healthcare, legal services, and even creative industries have also begun to embrace remote consultation, recognizing the value in connecting with clients and customers despite physical distances.

Nevertheless, while remote services offer remarkable advantages, there are challenges that both service providers and clients must navigate. Establishing trust and clear communication are crucial elements in remote consulting. Building trust without face-to-face interaction demands enhanced communication skills, reliable platforms, and a robust system to ensure the security and confidentiality of shared information.

Furthermore, the absence of physical presence can sometimes lead to difficulties in understanding nuanced issues or misinterpretations. Thus, developing effective strategies for remote interaction, including the use of video conferencing, advanced collaboration tools, and comprehensive documentation, becomes paramount in overcoming these obstacles.

As technology continues to evolve, the landscape of remote services and consulting will undoubtedly evolve as well. Innovations in artificial intelligence, augmented reality, and virtual reality may further enhance the remote consultation experience, providing more immersive and interactive solutions.

In conclusion, the realm of remote services and consulting is an ever-expanding and evolving frontier, offering unparalleled opportunities for professionals and businesses. Embracing this trend requires a commitment to effective communication, technological adaptation, and a willingness to explore innovative solutions. The future of remote services and consulting is promising, promising an era of increased connectivity, accessibility, and collaboration across boundaries and borders.

Chapter 20: Virtual Events and Webinars

Virtual events and webinars have transformed the landscape of communication, education, and networking. They've become an integral part of our modern world, especially with the rapid advancements in technology and the need for remote connectivity. These platforms offer a unique and convenient way for individuals and organizations to connect, share knowledge, and engage with audiences from all corners of the globe.

One of the most striking aspects of virtual events and webinars is their versatility. They cater to a wide range of purposes, from educational seminars and workshops to corporate meetings, product launches, and even entertainment events. The flexibility they offer in terms of content and format is remarkable, allowing hosts to customize the experience to suit their specific goals and the preferences of their audience.

From the perspective of an organizer or a presenter, the process of setting up a virtual event or webinar involves meticulous planning. This includes defining the objectives, selecting the right platform, creating engaging content, and ensuring a seamless technological setup. The success of these events often hinges on the quality of content, speakers, and the overall user experience. Therefore, much attention is given to creating compelling presentations, interactive sessions, and opportunities for audience engagement.

Audience engagement is a vital aspect of virtual events. While physical presence is absent, various tools are employed to keep attendees actively participating. These tools can range from live polls, Q&A sessions, interactive chats, breakout rooms, and even virtual networking opportunities. The aim is to make the event interactive, fostering a sense of community and involvement among the participants.

The technological aspect is a cornerstone of virtual events. The evolution of various platforms and software solutions has made hosting and participating in these events seamless. Video conferencing tools, webinar platforms, and event management software have advanced significantly, offering features that simulate the experience of in-person events while adding unique capabilities that are only possible in a virtual environment.

Moreover, the accessibility and inclusivity of virtual events are noteworthy. They break geographical barriers, enabling attendees from different parts of the world to join without the need for travel. This not only reduces costs but also allows for a more diverse audience. Additionally, it promotes inclusivity for individuals who might have limitations or difficulties attending physical events due to various reasons.

On the flip side, virtual events also present challenges. The absence of in-person interaction can sometimes lead to a lack of personal connection and engagement. Technical glitches or internet connectivity issues might disrupt the flow of the event. Ensuring that the virtual setup is user-friendly and that attendees feel connected and valued can be challenging.

Looking to the future, virtual events and webinars are likely to continue evolving. As technology advances, we can expect even more immersive and interactive experiences. The integration of virtual reality (VR) and augmented reality (AR) could offer a more lifelike environment, further blurring the line between physical and virtual spaces.

In conclusion, virtual events and webinars have become a fundamental part of our modern world, offering a flexible, accessible, and diverse means of communication and connection. As they continue to evolve, they will undoubtedly play an increasingly significant role in various fields, shaping the way we communicate, learn, and engage with one another.

Chapter 21: SEO and Digital Marketing Earnings

Search Engine Optimization (SEO) and Digital Marketing have become integral components of the modern business landscape. As businesses increasingly rely on the internet to reach their target audience, the demand for SEO and digital marketing services has grown significantly. In this narrative response, we'll explore the earnings potential in the SEO and digital marketing industry, taking into account various factors that influence income.

1. The Growth of the Industry:

The field of digital marketing and SEO has seen explosive growth over the past few years. With more businesses recognizing the importance of a strong online presence, there's a growing need for professionals who can help them navigate the digital landscape. This growth has created numerous opportunities for individuals and agencies to provide SEO and digital marketing services.

2. Factors Influencing Earnings:

Skill and Expertise:

One of the primary factors determining earnings in the SEO and digital marketing industry is the level of skill and expertise. Professionals who possess a deep understanding of SEO techniques, content marketing, social media marketing, and paid advertising are often able to command higher fees for their services. As they consistently produce results for their clients, they build a reputation that can lead to more lucrative opportunities.

Location:

Geographical location plays a significant role in earnings. In major metropolitan areas and regions with a high concentration of businesses, digital marketing professionals often have access to a larger pool of potential clients. This increased demand for services can translate into higher earnings. However, the cost of living and competition in these areas may also be higher, which can affect the bottom line.

Experience:

Experience is a key driver of earnings in the digital marketing and SEO industry. Entry-level professionals typically earn less than those with years of experience. As you gain practical experience and a proven track record of successful campaigns, your ability to command higher rates or salaries increases. Experienced professionals are often sought after for their insights and problem-solving abilities.

Specialization:

Specialization within the digital marketing field can significantly impact earnings. Professionals who specialize in niche areas such as e-commerce SEO, content marketing, or PPC (Pay-Per-Click) advertising can often command higher rates due to their specialized knowledge. Clients seeking specific expertise are willing to pay a premium for professionals who can deliver targeted results.

3. **Income Streams in SEO and Digital Marketing:**

Freelancing:

Many individuals in the SEO and digital marketing industry choose to work as freelancers. Freelancers have the flexibility to set their rates, choose their clients, and determine their workload. The earnings of freelancers can vary widely, depending on factors like their expertise, reputation, and the projects they undertake. Some successful freelancers can earn six-figure incomes or more annually.

Agency Work:

Working for a digital marketing agency is another common path. Agencies often have a diverse portfolio of clients and offer a structured work environment. Digital marketing professionals in agencies may earn a fixed salary, which varies based on experience and the size and reputation of the agency. Bonuses or commissions for successful campaigns can also contribute to overall earnings.

In-House Positions:

Many businesses, especially larger corporations, hire in-house digital marketing and SEO professionals. These positions often come with competitive salaries and benefits. In-house professionals may focus on the marketing efforts of a single company, which can provide a stable and predictable income. Earnings in in-house roles can range from mid-five figures to high six figures, depending on the size of the company and the role's level of responsibility.

Affiliate Marketing:

Some individuals in the digital marketing industry earn income through affiliate marketing. This involves promoting products or services through affiliate links and earning a commission on sales generated through those links. Successful affiliate marketers can generate significant passive income, but it often requires a great deal of time and effort to build a substantial revenue stream.

Consulting:

Consulting is another avenue for experienced digital marketing and SEO professionals. Consultants offer their expertise and advice to businesses looking to improve their online presence. They can charge premium rates for their strategic guidance, and their earnings are often tied to the results they help their clients achieve.

4. Income Potential in Different Roles:

Entry-Level SEO/Digital Marketing Professional:

Professionals in entry-level roles can expect to earn salaries that typically range from $35,000 to $60,000 per year, depending on factors such as location and the size of the employer. These roles often involve assisting with the execution of digital marketing campaigns, such as managing social media accounts, conducting keyword research, and creating content.

Mid-Level Digital Marketing/SEO Specialist:

Mid-level specialists with a few years of experience can earn salaries in the range of $60,000 to $100,000 per year. They are often responsible for managing entire digital marketing campaigns, including SEO efforts, content creation, and paid advertising. Salary levels can vary significantly based on experience and the scope of responsibilities.

Digital Marketing/SEO Manager:

Professionals who take on management roles can earn salaries in the range of $80,000 to $150,000 or more, depending on their experience and the size of the company. These roles involve overseeing digital marketing teams, creating and implementing strategies, and reporting on campaign performance.

Freelance Digital Marketers and SEO Specialists:

Freelancers have the potential to earn income that varies widely. Those with the right skills and reputation can charge hourly rates ranging from $50 to $200 or more. Annual earnings for successful freelancers can range from $50,000 to well into six figures, depending on the number and scale of projects they take on.

Digital Marketing Agency Professionals:

Salaries within digital marketing agencies depend on the specific role and the agency's size and reputation. Entry-level positions might start at around $40,000 to $60,000, while experienced account managers or directors can earn anywhere from $70,000 to $150,000 or more. Agency professionals may also receive performance-based bonuses.

In-House Digital Marketing/SEO Roles:

In-house professionals can earn competitive salaries, often ranging from $60,000 to $150,000 or more. Larger companies in major metropolitan areas tend to offer higher salaries. Some specialized roles in highly competitive industries may even command salaries in the high six figures or more.

5. Income Growth and Long-Term Prospects:

The digital marketing and SEO industry offers significant potential for income growth over time. As professionals gain experience, build a network, and achieve consistent results, their earning potential can increase substantially. Here are some factors that contribute to long-term income growth:

Reputation and Portfolio:

Building a strong reputation in the industry and showcasing a portfolio of successful campaigns can lead to more significant and high-paying opportunities. Clients and employers often seek out professionals with a proven track record of delivering results.

Continuing Education:

The digital marketing landscape is continuously evolving. Professionals who invest in ongoing education and stay updated on the latest trends and technologies are better positioned to provide value to clients or employers. They can command higher rates for their up-to-date knowledge and skills.

Specialization:

Specializing in a particular aspect of digital marketing or SEO, such as voice search optimization, video marketing, or local SEO, can make you a sought-after expert in your field. Specialized professionals can often charge premium rates for their expertise.

Entrepreneurship:

Some professionals choose to start their own digital marketing agencies or consulting businesses. While entrepreneurship involves greater risk, successful entrepreneurs have the potential to earn substantial income as they build their client base and scale their businesses.

Challenges and Considerations:

While the earnings potential in the digital marketing and SEO industry is significant, there are challenges and considerations to keep in mind:

Market Saturation:

The industry is becoming increasingly competitive. As more individuals enter the field, competition for clients and jobs intensifies. Standing out in a crowded market requires unique skills, a solid track record, and a differentiated approach to marketing oneself or one's services.

Constant Learning and Adaptability:

The digital marketing landscape is ever-evolving, with new algorithms, technologies, and trends emerging regularly. Professionals need to stay abreast of these changes, which often requires continuous learning and adaptation to remain competitive.

Client Expectations and Results:

Clients often have high expectations for the results they expect from their digital marketing efforts. Meeting or exceeding these expectations is crucial for retaining clients and securing new ones. Continuous performance and tangible results are essential for long-term success.

Work-Life Balance:

The nature of the industry, especially for freelancers and entrepreneurs, can sometimes blur the lines between work and personal life. Balancing a heavy workload and meeting deadlines while maintaining a healthy work-life balance is a challenge that many in the industry face.

In conclusion, the earnings potential in the SEO and digital marketing industry is substantial and varied, influenced by factors such as skill, experience, specialization, location, and the chosen career path, whether it's freelancing, agency work, in-house positions, affiliate marketing, or consulting. With the right skills, dedication, and adaptability, individuals in this field have the opportunity to build a successful and lucrative career.

Earnings can range from entry-level salaries in the mid-five figures to high six figures or more for seasoned professionals, consultants, or entrepreneurs. While the industry presents numerous opportunities for growth and financial success, it's essential to navigate the challenges and continuously evolve to remain competitive in this dynamic and ever-changing field.

Chapter 22: Remote Data Entry and Microtasks

In the ever-evolving landscape of modern work, remote data entry and microtasks have become integral components of various industries, particularly in the digital realm. The advent of the internet and technological advancements has not only transformed the way we communicate but has also revolutionized how businesses operate, manage information, and handle tasks. Remote data entry and microtasks are among the many aspects that have experienced a substantial shift due to these advancements.

1. Remote Data Entry:

Remote data entry involves the inputting of information into computer systems or databases from a location separate from the physical office. This method has gained immense popularity due to its flexibility and the ability to access a global pool of talent. Individuals can perform data entry tasks from the comfort of their homes, which not only saves commuting time but also allows for a better work-life balance.

Advantages of Remote Data Entry:

- **Flexibility:** Working remotely provides flexibility in terms of working hours and location. This flexibility is a major attraction for many individuals seeking work opportunities.

- **Cost-Efficiency:** Employers can save on overhead costs associated with maintaining physical office spaces, as they can hire remote workers without needing to provide dedicated office space.

- **Global Talent Pool:** Companies can tap into a diverse talent pool and potentially hire individuals from across the globe, allowing access to a wider range of skills and experiences.

- **Work-Life Balance:** Remote data entry allows for a better work-life balance. Individuals can set their schedules and work in an environment they find comfortable and productive.

2. Microtasks:

Microtasks, on the other hand, refer to small, often repetitive tasks that are fragmented from larger projects. These tasks are typically well-suited for remote work and are commonly found in various industries, such as data processing, content moderation, transcription, image tagging, and more. Companies use specialized platforms or tools to break down complex tasks into smaller, manageable units to be completed by a distributed workforce.

Advantages of Microtasks:

- **Scalability:** Microtasks can be easily divided and distributed among a large number of workers, allowing companies to handle a substantial volume of work efficiently.

- **Efficiency:** Breaking down larger projects into smaller, more manageable tasks often leads to increased efficiency. Workers can focus on specific elements, which can lead to quicker completion and higher accuracy.

- **Cost-Effective:** Microtasking allows companies to pay workers per task completed, making it cost-effective for handling routine, time-consuming tasks without the need for full-time employees.

- **Diversity in Tasks:** Workers have the opportunity to engage in diverse tasks, which can be intellectually stimulating and prevent monotony in their work.

Challenges of Remote Data Entry and Microtasks:

While remote data entry and microtasks offer numerous advantages, there are challenges associated with these work structures.

- **Isolation and Communication:** Remote work can be isolating, leading to difficulties in communication and collaboration. Clear communication channels and efficient tools are essential to overcome these challenges.
- **Quality Control:** Ensuring the quality and accuracy of work can be a challenge, especially in microtasks where each piece might be completed by different workers. Implementing rigorous quality control measures is vital.
- **Security Concerns:** Handling sensitive data remotely can pose security risks. Companies must invest in robust security measures to safeguard information.
- **Fair Compensation:** Ensuring fair compensation for remote workers, especially in microtasks where pay might be per task, is crucial for retaining a skilled and motivated workforce.

The Future of Remote Data Entry and Microtasks:

The future of remote data entry and microtasks seems promising, given the growing trend of remote work and the increasing sophistication of task allocation algorithms and platforms. With advancements in artificial intelligence and machine learning, some routine tasks might be automated, allowing human workers to focus on more complex, higher-value tasks. Additionally, the integration of blockchain technology may address issues of trust, security, and fair compensation in remote work environments.

In conclusion, remote data entry and microtasks have become integral in the modern work landscape, offering flexibility and scalability while presenting challenges that need to be addressed. The future will likely see further evolution and refinement in these areas, enabling more efficient, secure, and rewarding remote work opportunities for a global workforce.

Chapter 23: Writing and Publishing Earnings

Writing and publishing earnings can be a dynamic and diverse landscape, influenced by multiple factors that shape an author's financial success. The income an author generates from their writing can vary significantly, ranging from modest to substantial, and is influenced by various aspects such as the type of writing, the publishing method, book sales, royalties, advances, and other streams of income.

For many writers, especially those who are starting, income from their craft may not be substantial. Often, new authors might face a period of investing more time and effort into writing than the financial return it provides. When starting, authors may see little to no income as they focus on building their craft, completing manuscripts, and trying to secure a publishing deal.

Traditional publishing typically involves submitting a manuscript to literary agents or publishing houses. If accepted, authors may receive an advance against future royalties. These advances can range widely, from a few thousand dollars to several million, but they usually represent a portion of the expected royalties from book sales. It's important to note that these advances are usually paid in installments – upon signing the publishing contract, upon delivery and acceptance of the manuscript, and upon publication.

Royalties from book sales also contribute to an author's income in traditional publishing. The standard royalty rates for authors typically range between 8% to 15% of the book's retail price, though these rates can vary based on the format of the book (e-book, hardcover, paperback) and the terms of the publishing contract. However, it's crucial to understand that these royalties are paid after the publisher has recouped the advance paid to the author.

On the other hand, self-publishing has become a popular avenue for many writers due to the ease of accessibility and the potential for higher royalties. Self-published authors retain more control over their work and may earn higher royalties per sale, which can range from 35% to 70% of the book's price, depending on the platform used and distribution channels.

Furthermore, the success of an author's earnings is greatly influenced by the book's performance in the market. Factors such as genre, marketing efforts, the author's platform, the book's reviews, and word-of-mouth play significant roles in determining book sales and, subsequently, the earnings an author accrues.

Apart from book sales, authors can explore additional income streams such as speaking engagements, teaching writing workshops, freelance writing, merchandise related to their books, and even adaptations of their work into movies or television series, which can substantially contribute to their overall earnings.

It's important to recognize that while some authors achieve significant financial success, many authors, even talented and prolific ones, might struggle to earn a full-time income solely from their writing. Many successful authors supplement their writing income with other jobs or freelance work, especially early in their careers.

In conclusion, the earnings from writing and publishing are diverse and can vary greatly. While some authors may achieve substantial financial success, for many, it's a gradual process that involves a mix of factors, patience, perseverance, and, in some cases, additional income streams to sustain a career in writing. Success in the literary world often involves not just talent and hard work but also an understanding of the industry, persistence, and adaptability to changing market trends.

Chapter 24: Language Teaching and Translation Services

Language Teaching and Translation Services play an integral role in bridging communication gaps and fostering understanding between diverse cultures and linguistic communities. These services are pivotal in today's globalized world, facilitating cross-cultural interactions, trade, diplomacy, education, and numerous other aspects of human interaction.

1. Language Teaching:

Language teaching encompasses a vast array of methodologies and approaches aimed at instructing individuals in acquiring proficiency in a particular language. Whether it's teaching a second language to non-native speakers or even enhancing proficiency in the native language, language teaching services come in various forms and are tailored to meet specific needs.

2. Importance of Language Teaching:

Enhanced Communication: Effective language teaching allows individuals to communicate and interact more fluently with a broader range of people, enabling them to participate more actively in various spheres of life, from social interactions to professional endeavors.

- **Cultural Understanding:** Language teaching isn't just about grammar and vocabulary. It also incorporates cultural nuances, idiomatic expressions, and historical contexts, providing a deeper understanding of the culture associated with the language.
- **Global Opportunities:** Proficiency in multiple languages opens up a multitude of opportunities in diverse fields such as business, education, international relations, and tourism. In the global job market, multilingual skills are highly valued.

3. **Methods of Language Teaching:**
   - **Communicative Approach:** This method emphasizes real-life communication and situational language use, encouraging students to speak and interact in the target language.
   - **Direct Method:** Focuses on teaching the target language without using the students' native language. It promotes the idea of immersion in the language.

- **Audio-lingual Method:** Emphasizes repetition and habit formation, often using drills and structured dialogues.
- **Task-Based Learning:** Learning is centered around completing tasks or projects using the target language, making it more practical and applicable.

4. Translation Services:

Translation services involve the conversion of written or spoken content from one language to another, ensuring the conveyed message maintains its original meaning, tone, and context. Translators serve as linguistic mediators, preserving the essence of the original text while making it accessible to a different audience.

5. Importance of Translation Services:
- **Global Communication:** In an interconnected world, translation facilitates communication across borders and languages, enabling the sharing of information, ideas, and knowledge.
- **Business and Commerce:** Translation is vital in global business transactions, enabling companies to reach a wider audience and establish a presence in diverse markets.

- **Cultural Exchange:** Through translation, literary works, academic research, and cultural pieces can be shared and appreciated globally, fostering cross-cultural understanding and appreciation.

6. **Translation Methods and Challenges:**
    - **Literal vs. Dynamic Translation:** Literal translation adheres closely to the original text, while dynamic translation focuses on conveying the meaning rather than the exact words.
    - **Cultural Nuances:** Translators often encounter challenges related to idiomatic expressions, cultural references, and humor that might not directly translate, requiring a nuanced approach.
    - **Specialized Fields:** Technical, legal, medical, and academic translations require expertise in the specific field, demanding deep knowledge in both languages and subject matter.

7. **Integration of Language Teaching and Translation:**

These two services often intersect, especially in language learning environments. Incorporating translation exercises into language teaching helps students comprehend the nuances between languages and aids in better understanding and application of learned vocabulary and grammar rules.

Language teaching may also involve translation as a tool for learning. It helps students grasp the structures and differences between their native language and the one they are learning, enhancing their overall understanding and fluency.

In conclusion, Language Teaching and Translation Services are invaluable in breaking down language barriers and fostering global understanding. They are not only instrumental in facilitating communication but also in preserving and sharing the diversity of languages and cultures worldwide. The integration of these services plays a crucial role in creating a more interconnected and harmonious global community.

Chapter 25: Online Real Estate and Property Sales

The world of real estate has undergone a significant transformation with the emergence of online platforms for property sales. The advent of the internet and the subsequent development of digital technologies have revolutionized the way real estate transactions take place. This transformation has reshaped the industry, offering both buyers and sellers an array of benefits, while also presenting new challenges and opportunities.

In the not-so-distant past, buying or selling property typically involved visiting multiple locations, meeting with real estate agents, and poring over classifieds in newspapers or real estate magazines. It was a time-consuming process that often required extensive footwork and reliance on the expertise of a few select professionals.

However, with the advent of online real estate sales, the landscape has dramatically changed. The internet has become the primary marketplace for real estate transactions. Various online platforms and websites now host a vast array of properties, allowing potential buyers to explore, compare, and evaluate numerous options from the comfort of their own homes.

One of the fundamental advantages of online property sales is the accessibility and convenience it offers. Buyers can browse through a wide range of properties at any time of the day, from almost any location with an internet connection. This means that the limitations of physical distance and time constraints no longer hinder the property search process. Moreover, the detailed information available online, including photographs, virtual tours, floor plans, and descriptions, offers a comprehensive understanding of the property even before a physical visit.

Sellers also benefit significantly from online real estate sales. They can showcase their properties to a much broader audience, transcending geographical boundaries. Online platforms allow for efficient marketing and exposure, enabling sellers to reach a larger pool of potential buyers. Additionally, the ability to upload photos, videos, and detailed descriptions can help highlight the best features of the property, attracting more interest and inquiries.

The use of technology in online real estate sales has further revolutionized the industry. Features like 3D virtual tours, drone photography for aerial views, and interactive floor plans have enhanced the way buyers explore and experience properties. These technological advancements provide a more immersive and realistic understanding of the property, reducing the need for multiple physical visits and ultimately expediting the decision-making process for buyers.

Moreover, the integration of data analytics and artificial intelligence has also played a pivotal role in online real estate sales. These tools help in market analysis, pricing strategies, and predictive modeling, empowering both buyers and sellers with valuable insights. For buyers, these technologies assist in comparative market analysis, giving them a clearer picture of property values in different areas. Sellers, on the other hand, can use these tools to price their properties more accurately and competitively.

However, while online real estate sales offer numerous advantages, there are also challenges that come with this shift. The reliance on digital platforms raises concerns regarding the authenticity and accuracy of the information provided. Misleading or incomplete information can potentially lead to misunderstandings and complications during the buying process.

Furthermore, despite the convenience of viewing properties online, the physical inspection remains a crucial aspect of the purchasing process. Online platforms may provide a comprehensive overview, but the sensory experience of physically visiting a property—feeling the space, assessing the neighborhood, and understanding the surrounding environment—is something that cannot be entirely replicated digitally.

Another challenge is the abundance of information available online, which can sometimes overwhelm buyers. Sorting through countless property listings and navigating various platforms might become daunting, and there's a risk of important details being overlooked or undervalued.

The human element in real estate transactions is another aspect that could be impacted by the shift to online sales. The personal touch and guidance provided by real estate agents in understanding the market, negotiating deals, and facilitating transactions may be diminished in an online-centric environment.

Nonetheless, real estate professionals have adapted to this changing landscape, utilizing technology to their advantage. Many agents have expanded their online presence, leveraging social media, virtual staging, and interactive tools to engage with clients and showcase properties effectively.

The future of online real estate sales continues to evolve with advancements in technology. Concepts such as blockchain for property transactions, virtual reality for immersive property tours, and further advancements in artificial intelligence are likely to shape the industry in the years to come. These innovations hold the potential to address current challenges and further streamline the buying and selling process.

In conclusion, online real estate and property sales have reshaped the way transactions are conducted, offering convenience, accessibility, and a vast array of options to both buyers and sellers. While it presents challenges, the integration of technology and innovative approaches have and will continue to redefine the real estate industry, promising an exciting and dynamic future for all involved.

Chapter 26: Virtual Assistant Development and AI Opportunities

The landscape of virtual assistant development and AI opportunities is an ever-evolving canvas, continually shaped by technological advancements, societal needs, and the quest for innovation. In recent years, the proliferation of artificial intelligence (AI) has brought about remarkable advancements in virtual assistant technology, transforming the way we interact with machines and access information.

At the core of this evolution lies the development of virtual assistants, AI-driven systems designed to understand and respond to human queries, perform tasks, and adapt to user needs. Companies and developers have been drawn to this field due to the potential for vast applications in various industries. The creation of virtual assistants involves a combination of natural language processing (NLP), machine learning, and data analysis to comprehend and generate human-like responses.

These assistants, such as Siri, Alexa, Google Assistant, and others, have become integral parts of our daily lives, serving functions ranging from answering questions, managing schedules, setting reminders, and controlling smart home devices. The market's expansion continues as businesses recognize the value of virtual assistants in customer service, streamlining operations, and enhancing user experiences.

AI opportunities in this field are multifaceted. From a developmental perspective, engineers, software developers, and data scientists have vast prospects to contribute to the enhancement and evolution of virtual assistants. They work on refining algorithms, improving language understanding, and expanding the capabilities of these assistants to handle complex tasks efficiently.

Moreover, the integration of AI into virtual assistants is not limited to consumer-oriented applications. The healthcare industry, for instance, benefits from AI-driven assistants capable of analyzing vast amounts of medical data, assisting in diagnostics, and providing personalized patient care.

Furthermore, the adoption of AI in virtual assistants has been influential in other industries like finance, education, and entertainment. AI-powered tools aid financial institutions in risk assessment and fraud detection, while educational institutions use them to personalize learning experiences for students. In the entertainment sector, AI contributes to content recommendation systems, enhancing user engagement and satisfaction.

The future prospects for AI and virtual assistants are promising. Continued advancements in AI technologies, including deep learning and neural networks, are driving the evolution of more sophisticated and context-aware virtual assistants. The emergence of emotional intelligence in these systems, enabling them to understand and respond to human emotions, is on the horizon. This development could revolutionize the way we interact with technology, creating more personalized and empathetic experiences.

However, challenges persist, including privacy concerns, ethical considerations, and the need to mitigate biases in AI systems. As AI becomes more pervasive, addressing these issues becomes increasingly critical to ensure responsible and ethical use of these technologies.

In conclusion, the development of virtual assistants and the vast array of AI opportunities they present is a testament to the potential of technology to reshape our world.

The continuous innovation in this field offers immense promise, and as developers and innovators continue to push the boundaries of AI, the potential applications and impact on society are boundless. The evolution of virtual assistants is not just a technological advancement but a redefinition of how we interact with and benefit from intelligent machines, reshaping the very fabric of our daily lives.

Chapter 27: Building and Monetizing Online Communities

Building and monetizing online communities represents a fascinating intersection of human connection and entrepreneurship, where the digital landscape becomes a platform for individuals with shared interests or goals to come together, engage, and interact. The evolution of the internet has facilitated the creation and growth of these communities, which can range from social media groups and forums to specialized platforms dedicated to various niches.

The foundation of a successful online community lies in the ability to foster genuine connections and provide value to its members. Building such a community requires a strategic approach that starts with identifying a common interest, need, or passion that can unite individuals. Understanding the target audience is pivotal – what drives them, what challenges they face, and what they seek from a community.

Content plays a crucial role in creating and maintaining engagement. Whether it's informative articles, discussion threads, multimedia content, or interactive activities, the content needs to be relevant and compelling. This not only attracts members but also keeps them coming back. It's about building a space where members feel heard, understood, and where their contributions are valued.

A sense of community is nurtured through active participation and fostering meaningful discussions. Moderation is key to maintain a positive and respectful environment. Encouraging user-generated content, initiating discussions, and acknowledging member contributions are pivotal in making the community thrive.

As the community grows and members become more engaged, opportunities for monetization start to emerge. Monetization strategies can take various forms. One common method is through advertisements and sponsorships. However, these need to be balanced carefully to avoid overwhelming the user experience and turning away members.

Another method is through subscription models or premium content. Offering exclusive content, features, or access to a more in-depth experience can entice members to upgrade to a paid subscription. The content or features offered must be valuable enough to warrant the subscription fee while ensuring the free content remains enticing to attract new users.

E-commerce within the community is another way to monetize. Creating a marketplace within the community where members can buy, sell, or trade items related to the community's interest can generate revenue. This not only provides a revenue stream but also enhances the community's value by being a one-stop destination for its members.

Moreover, partnerships and collaborations with relevant brands or businesses can be beneficial. By leveraging the community's influence and engagement, partnerships can offer exclusive deals, products, or services to members while generating revenue through affiliate marketing or collaborations.

An often underestimated aspect of monetization is data and analytics. Understanding the community's behavior, interests, and engagement patterns can be incredibly valuable for businesses seeking insights into their target market. This information can be packaged and sold to relevant businesses for market research or advertising purposes.

While monetization is a key aspect, it's crucial to maintain the integrity and authenticity of the community. Balancing the commercial aspect with the community's original purpose and value is essential. Ensuring that the members feel they are part of a genuine, supportive environment is vital to sustain the community in the long run.

In conclusion, building and monetizing online communities requires a delicate balance between fostering genuine connections, providing valuable content, and implementing monetization strategies that don't compromise the community's integrity. When done successfully, these communities can become a hub for engagement, information sharing, and commerce, benefiting both the members and the community owners.

Chapter 28: Fundraising and Crowdfunding Initiatives

Fundraising and crowdfunding initiatives are critical components of modern ventures and projects. They serve as dynamic mechanisms to garner financial support, rally communities, and propel innovative ideas, social causes, and entrepreneurial endeavors. The evolution of fundraising and crowdfunding has been transformative, reshaping the ways individuals, organizations, and businesses procure resources, engage supporters, and bring their visions to fruition.

1. The Concept of Fundraising and Crowdfunding

At its core, fundraising is the practice of soliciting financial contributions or other resources to support a particular cause or initiative. Traditionally, it was carried out through direct solicitations, events, and grant applications. Over time, fundraising techniques have expanded and diversified, incorporating various strategies, from traditional methods to leveraging modern technologies.

Crowdfunding, a relatively newer concept, has revolutionized fundraising dynamics. It involves reaching out to a broader audience through online platforms, inviting smaller contributions from a large number of individuals or groups. This approach democratizes funding by allowing a more extensive pool of contributors to participate in supporting an idea or cause.

2. Types of Fundraising and Crowdfunding Initiatives

Fundraising initiatives span a broad spectrum, catering to diverse purposes and audiences. Non-profit organizations engage in fundraising to support charitable causes, while entrepreneurs seek funding for startup ventures. Political campaigns rely on fundraising to finance electoral pursuits, while individuals might seek support for personal causes, medical expenses, or creative projects.

Similarly, crowdfunding initiatives vary in nature and purpose. Reward-based crowdfunding, where contributors receive incentives or rewards for their donations, has been popularized by platforms like Kickstarter and Indiegogo. Equity crowdfunding involves raising capital by offering equity or ownership stakes in a company. Donation-based crowdfunding focuses on gathering funds for charitable causes or personal needs without any expectation of returns.

3. The Impact of Technology on Fundraising

Technological advancements have significantly reshaped the landscape of fundraising and crowdfunding. Online platforms have emerged as pivotal tools for reaching a global audience, streamlining the donation process, and facilitating engagement with contributors. Social media channels serve as powerful catalysts, enabling campaigns to go viral and gain widespread attention.

The accessibility and ease of use associated with online platforms have democratized fundraising, empowering individuals and organizations to create campaigns independently. This accessibility has reduced barriers to entry and expanded the reach of fundraising efforts, enabling even small-scale initiatives to gain visibility and support.

Moreover, the data-driven nature of online fundraising platforms allows for analytics and insights, helping campaign organizers to refine their strategies and target their efforts more effectively. Understanding donor behavior and preferences assists in crafting compelling campaigns, optimizing messaging, and enhancing overall engagement.

4. Strategies for Successful Fundraising and Crowdfunding

Crafting a successful fundraising or crowdfunding initiative requires a strategic approach. A compelling narrative is crucial—telling a compelling story that resonates emotionally with potential donors or contributors. A narrative that conveys the impact of the initiative and how contributions will make a difference can significantly increase engagement and support.

Transparency and accountability are equally vital. Donors want to trust that their contributions will be used effectively. Providing clear information on how funds will be utilized and maintaining transparency throughout the process builds trust and credibility, encouraging continued support.

Timing and promotion play critical roles in the success of a campaign. Understanding the target audience and the best channels to reach them is key. Leveraging social media, email marketing, and other online tools effectively can expand the campaign's reach and visibility.

Engagement and fostering a sense of community around the cause or initiative are essential. Responding to donors, updating them on the progress of the campaign, and expressing gratitude for their contributions help in building a loyal and supportive community.

5. Challenges and Opportunities in Fundraising and Crowdfunding

Despite the myriad benefits, fundraising and crowdfunding also present challenges. The competitive landscape of online platforms means that standing out among numerous campaigns requires creative and innovative approaches. Campaign fatigue, where donors are inundated with multiple solicitations, can also pose a challenge.

Moreover, establishing trust in an online environment, where fraudulent or misleading campaigns exist, is crucial. A single high-profile scam can potentially erode trust across the entire platform, affecting genuine initiatives.

Legislation and regulations around fundraising, especially in the context of equity crowdfunding, vary across different regions and can be complex to navigate. Compliance with legal requirements and ensuring that all regulations are adhered to is essential.

However, amidst these challenges lie significant opportunities. The vast potential of online fundraising and crowdfunding remains largely untapped. Platforms continue to evolve, offering new features, improved user experiences, and expanded functionalities that can further enhance campaign success.

6. The Future of Fundraising and Crowdfunding

Looking ahead, the future of fundraising and crowdfunding seems promising. Technology will continue to be a driving force, with advancements in AI, blockchain, and other emerging technologies likely to reshape the landscape further. These innovations hold the potential to increase security, transparency, and efficiency in fundraising efforts.

Personalization and customization are expected to play a more prominent role, tailoring campaigns to specific donor preferences and behaviors. Hyper-targeting and precision in reaching potential contributors may become more prevalent, amplifying the impact of campaigns.

Collaborations between traditional financial institutions and crowdfunding platforms might grow, enabling a broader array of financial services to support fundraising initiatives. Partnerships that merge the benefits of both worlds—traditional finance and modern crowdfunding—could further expand the opportunities available to fundraisers.

In conclusion, fundraising and crowdfunding initiatives have evolved significantly, revolutionizing the way individuals, organizations, and businesses source financial support for their endeavors. With the advent of online platforms, these mechanisms have become more accessible, democratizing fundraising and allowing a more extensive range of causes and ventures to find support. While challenges persist, the future appears promising, with continued advancements in technology, regulatory improvements, and evolving strategies set to shape the landscape of fundraising and crowdfunding for years to come.

Chapter 29: Remote Health and Wellness Services

In the contemporary landscape of health and wellness, the advent of remote services has revolutionized the way individuals access and engage with healthcare, marking a significant shift in the delivery of medical care, fitness regimens, mental health support, and overall well-being management. This paradigm shift has been accelerated by the convergence of technology, changing societal norms, and the global events that necessitated a rethinking of traditional healthcare practices.

Remote health and wellness services encompass a broad spectrum, incorporating telemedicine, virtual consultations, digital fitness programs, mental health apps, and various other online platforms designed to provide holistic support to individuals in pursuit of healthier lives. This evolution in healthcare delivery transcends geographical barriers and time constraints, offering convenience, accessibility, and a level of personalization that was once unimaginable.

Telemedicine, one of the cornerstones of remote health services, has made healthcare more accessible than ever. It allows patients to consult healthcare providers remotely through video calls, phone calls, or secure messaging. This has proven to be a game-changer, especially for those with limited mobility, individuals in rural or underserved areas, and those seeking specialized care.

Moreover, the digital transformation has empowered individuals to take control of their well-being. Fitness and wellness apps, for instance, have democratized access to tailored workout routines, nutritional guidance, and mindfulness practices. These platforms offer personalized fitness plans, track progress, and sometimes even provide real-time feedback and support from certified trainers and health professionals, fostering a sense of accountability and motivation.

Mental health services have also seen a significant transition towards remote care. Online therapy sessions, mental health chatbots, and apps offering meditation and stress-relief techniques have become indispensable tools for many seeking support in managing their mental and emotional health. These platforms afford individuals the opportunity to seek help in a discreet, convenient manner, reducing the stigma often associated with mental health issues.

The integration of wearable technology has further propelled the remote health and wellness revolution. Smartwatches, fitness trackers, and health monitoring devices allow individuals to continuously track their health metrics such as heart rate, sleep patterns, physical activity, and even detect potential health issues. These devices not only provide real-time data but also sync seamlessly with various health apps, providing users with a comprehensive overview of their well-being.

Challenges do exist in the realm of remote health and wellness services. Issues of data security, the need for consistent internet access, and the potential for misdiagnosis or limited physical examination in remote consultations remain areas of concern. Additionally, ensuring equitable access to these technologies and services for all demographics and addressing digital literacy gaps are critical challenges that need to be navigated.

The evolution of remote health and wellness services is continually shaping the future of healthcare. The amalgamation of technology, healthcare expertise, and user-centered design is enhancing accessibility, personalization, and the overall quality of care. As the world progresses, the synergy between these remote services and in-person care will likely become more seamless, offering a comprehensive approach to health and wellness that transcends the limitations of traditional healthcare models. The ongoing innovation in this sphere holds the promise of transforming lives, making healthcare more efficient, effective, and, most importantly, more patient-centric.

Chapter 30: Reflection and Next Steps

Looking back on the past year, it's difficult not to feel overwhelmed by the whirlwind of experiences and the multitude of emotions that have colored this period. The sheer scale of events, both personal and global, has been nothing short of transformative. It's almost surreal to consider the journey traversed, with its peaks and valleys, moments of joy and profound challenges. As I sit back to contemplate the footsteps left behind, it's evident that every step taken has been a part of an intricate dance—sometimes graceful, sometimes stumbling, but always forward-moving.

The year began with a blend of anticipation and uncertainty. Hopes and aspirations intermingled with doubts, setting the tone for a year that would be defined by adaptation and resilience. Challenges emerged unexpectedly, yet each one presented an opportunity for growth. In hindsight, those hurdles now seem like essential building blocks that have contributed to my evolution.

There were personal milestones—moments of triumph and elation that sparkled against the backdrop of routine. They served as a reminder that even amidst chaos, there's space for celebration and gratitude. Friendships flourished, new connections were made, and bonds deepened, reminding me of the profound impact relationships have in shaping our lives.

The professional landscape experienced seismic shifts, redefining the way we work and interact. Adaptability became a cornerstone skill, and navigating through the ever-evolving paradigms demanded resilience and resourcefulness. It was a year of learning, unlearning, and relearning—the continual process of evolution.

The global canvas painted a picture of collective turmoil and resilience. Societal challenges, from health crises to environmental concerns, tested our mettle, compelling us to stand together and rethink our roles in shaping a better world. It was a reminder that we're interconnected, and our actions ripple across boundaries, impacting lives far beyond our immediate spheres.

Next Steps:

As I stand on the threshold of a new chapter, the question of "what's next?" resonates loudly. The reflective journey has paved the way for deliberate contemplation about the path forward. While the future remains veiled in uncertainty, the experiences of the past year have equipped me with resilience and insight to navigate the unknown.

The upcoming chapter holds the promise of new beginnings and fresh challenges. It's a canvas waiting to be painted with intentions, aspirations, and goals—both personal and professional. There's an inherent excitement in the ambiguity of the unknown, a chance to embrace the unexpected and channel it into growth opportunities.

Self-improvement stands as a focal point. Reflecting on the past year has illuminated areas that could benefit from further development. Whether it's acquiring new skills, nurturing existing talents, or fostering a healthier lifestyle, the commitment to personal growth remains unwavering.

Professionally, the focus shifts towards honing expertise and exploring innovative avenues. Embracing change and adaptability will continue to be pillars in the ever-evolving work environment. Learning from past experiences, I aim to approach challenges with an open mind and a strategic perspective, leveraging lessons learned to achieve greater success.

Contributing to the greater good, both on a local and global scale, remains a driving force. The challenges of the world call for active participation, and as I move forward, a commitment to social responsibility and environmental consciousness will play an integral role in decision-making and actions.

The journey ahead is not just about setting goals but also about embracing the process, relishing every experience, and learning from each twist and turn. It's about staying true to the values that define who I am while remaining open to the opportunities that the universe presents.

In conclusion, the reflection on the past year has been instrumental in shaping the trajectory of the upcoming chapter. It's about learning from the past, embracing the present, and paving the way for an exciting and purposeful future—one that amalgamates personal growth, professional fulfillment, and a commitment to making a positive impact in the world. The journey continues, and as the pen hovers over the blank pages of the year to come, I am ready to script the next chapter with enthusiasm, resilience, and an unwavering spirit of adventure.

www.ingramcontent.com/pod-product-compliance
Lightning Source LLC
Chambersburg PA
CBHW082212290526
45794CB00009B/3514